TRADITIONAL CHINA

ASIAN CIVILIZATION

This series of interdisciplinary readings is designed to introduce the western reader to the distinctive components of Asian civilization—social order, political institutions, economic problems, and cultural milieu. Each set of paired volumes contrasts ancient and modern subjects; ageless tradition has been balanced by recent analysis to reveal historical continuity amid the unprecedented change occurring in Asia today.

James T. C. Liu, coeditor of this volume in the Asian Civilization series, is Professor of East Asian Studies and History, and Director of the East Asian Studies Program at Princeton University. He has written several books on traditional China, including *Ou-yuang Hsiu-n, An Eleventh-Century Neo-Confucianist.*

Coeditor **Wei-ming Tu** is Assistant Professor of East Asian Studies at Princeton University. He teaches courses on Confucianism and Chinese intellectual history and has written several articles in Chinese on the cultural identity of modern China.

TRADITIONAL CHINA

Edited by
James T. C. Liu and Wei-ming Tu

A SPECTRUM BOOK

C–13-926014-5
P–13-926006-4

Library of Congress Catalog Card Number 77-104855.

Printed in the United States of America.

Current printing (last number):
10 9 8 7 6 5 4 3 2 1

PRENTICE-HALL INTERNATIONAL, INC. (*London*)
PRENTICE-HALL OF AUSTRALIA, PTY. LTD. (*Sydney*)
PRENTICE-HALL OF CANADA, LTD. (*Toronto*)
PRENTICE-HALL OF INDIA PRIVATE LIMITED (*New Delhi*)
PRENTICE-HALL OF JAPAN, INC. (*Tokyo*)

CONTENTS

TRADITIONAL CHINA

INTRODUCTION

James T. C. Liu and Wei-ming Tu

No civilization in the world today has had a longer continuity than the Chinese. Having developed into a fairly high form as early as 4,000 years ago and gone through innumerable evolutionary changes, it has maintained down to the present century an amazing cultural stability and a distinct identity of its own. This unique fact speaks for itself, and cannot be ignored by anyone claiming to be interested in comparative civilizations, indeed in the history of mankind.

True, much of the old Chinese way of life is rapidly disappearing under unprecedented changes in the last few decades. No longer viable in the industrial world, many traits of the traditional culture have been picked as the targets of revolutionary attacks; destroyed by the successive waves of economic, social, and political upheavals; and discarded by the urgent drive toward radical modernization that reflects a fervent desire to catch up with the leading technological nations. Yet, paradoxical as it may seem, the traditional background still plays a significant part, much like an unseen hand, in steering revolutionary China, amid storm and stress, through uncharted waters. For no revolution, no matter how radical, can possibly eradicate certain national characteristics. And no change, no matter how uprooting, can possibly remove all cultural roots. On the one hand, China, already very different from what it was, will become even more so in the days ahead. On the other hand, it will always be China—neither in the reactionary sense of turning the clock back, which is impossible, nor in the stagnant sense of forever China or the unchanging East, which is nothing but a myth untrue even in bygone centuries, but in the dynamic sense of a long heritage in great flux. Much of significance from its past will somehow be integrated or embodied in the China of the future, whatever shape it may take.

The foregoing, though not wishful thinking, is admittedly an oversimplification. However, this is hardly the place to indulge in a lengthy discussion of theories of cultural change or to burden the readers with historical illustrations from Chinese or other civilizations. Perhaps a few random examples from the present may help to make the point. One of today's best sellers is the so-called Little Red Book or *The Quotations of Chairman Mao Tse-tung*. Regardless of the contents, the genre is certainly not new at all. Shortly after A.D. 1200, there was a compilation of the quotations of Chu Hsi, the founder of Neo-Confucianism. This compilation in turn had its roots in the most famous book in Chinese history: the *Analects,* sometimes translated as *The Sayings of Confucius.* Another example: Mainland China has in the last few years struggled with the difficult problem of how to reform the educational system. Much more serious than the vexing debates on curriculum, work-study plans, and the like is the basic problem of upward social mobility: who among the enormous population should have the privilege of education and thus the opportunity of joining the elite? How should the elite be trained so that they might hopefully have the interest of the common people at heart? In past centuries, the civil service examination system with its emphasis on Confucian classics and literary talents provided the answer. Now, some new system has to be forged.

It should be evident that traditional China is worth studying both for the intrinsic value of broadening one's mind through exposure to a great non-Western civilization and for the purpose of gaining some insight into this rapidly changing country on the other side of the Pacific. One would be well advised to read at least a good college text, a couple of source books or anthologies, and a few scholarly works that best represent this rigorously developing field of study. The present compilation can hardly pretend to serve as a substitute for any of these. In fact, it merely offers some introductory guideposts in the hope of arousing interest so that the reader may push on to something more substantive.

Even with this modest objective in mind, it has been no easy task to make selections that would illuminate this long and immensely complex civilization. The themes chosen can hardly claim to be consistently representative, for what was true in one century might not apply to the next. Nor are they sufficiently comprehensive, for in focusing on certain dimensions they tend to neglect others. Amidst these difficulties, we tried to adhere to the following: a schematic presentation that would introduce the salient features of Chinese civilization and their interrelationships.

Chapter 1, by one of the co-editors, Professor Liu, is a brief survey that seeks to show how various geographical, intellectual, and institutional factors interacted to keep the Chinese civilization integrated. But integration is not a constant and should not be confused with stagnation. Actually, in China many slow and incremental changes were modifying the tradition, while the tradition in turn modified these changes so that none would get out of bounds or undermine the pattern as a whole.

The geographic factors are further explained in Chapter 2 by Professor Spencer. The relative geographic isolation of China from other parts of Asia diminished the possibility of drastic intrusions that might upset the integration of the Chinese civilization. Within this integration, however, there were a variety of regional differences, again influenced by geographic conditions. Most important in this agricultural country is land. Contrary to popular misconception, the amount of arable land has been rather limited. Nor is the land in most places very fertile. These conditions have called for a tremendous emphasis upon human efforts and man-made improvements.

Professor Twitchett in Chapter 3 focuses upon a great turning point in the middle part of Chinese history, the T'ang (618–907) and the Sung (960–1279) period. With the decline of the aristocracy, the number of semi-servile tenants also decreased. From then on, the land was worked more and more by relatively free tenants as well as by independent peasants. Even more decisive than this change in social structure was a "great leap forward" in agricultural productivity through such efforts as land reclamation, improved farming techniques, new implements, and the introduction of an early-ripening variety of rice that made possible double-cropping in a year. It was this enormous increase in productivity that gave China its great wealth, so much more than any other country at the time and so impressive to Marco Polo in his travels there in the late thirteenth century.

What impressed Marco Polo even more than the prosperous countryside were the cities. At least a dozen of them were much larger than any city in Europe. However, as Professor Mote points out in Chapter 4, Marco Polo never understood that Chinese cities were qualitatively different from European cities. Both their structures and their functions were conditioned by the Chinese milieu. Most important, China had what may be described as an urban-rural continuum without a sharp cultural differentiation. In other words, these Chinese cities, great and small, were rooted in the basically rural society. This brilliant analysis is yet another way of showing how the Chinese civilization has been integrated.

Still, with so much wealth in the great cities, the question naturally arises: how did China fail to develop capitalism? The interpretation given by Professor Mote already offers one of the reasons. The late Professor Balazs in Chapter 5 suggests several other explanations such as the state monopolies, the official domination over the merchants, the preference to invest in land, the lack of security for individual enterprise, and the abundance of cheap labor that made machinery unnecessary.

Indeed the problem of why capitalism did not take place in China cannot be properly answered without knowing the social structure. In Chapter 3 by Professor Twitchett, we have already noted the decline of the aristocracy after the late T'ang and particularly from Sung on. Their successors were the professional bureaucrats who came up through the civil service examination system. Chapter 6, selected from Professor Ho's monumental work, shows that while traditional China did not have what we would call in the present century an "open society," it did have a pre-modern social structure remarkably close to it. Professor Ho defines it as "fluidity of status system." Even poor families who could manage to get by would send their intelligent boys to study in the hope of becoming officials. The merchant families were of course in a much more favorable position to prepare their sons for the competition. For them, it was not so important, so to speak, to make the next million of silver as it was to have the son become a high official. While the fluidity of status system may be an unfavorable factor in the lack of capitalistic development, it certainly had a most healthy effect on the Chinese ruling class as a whole. Through competitive examination, aspiring talent was recruited, while indulgent descendants of established families lost out. This insured a social circulation of new blood.

Professor Kracke in Chapter 7 goes on from the examination system to other admirable features of the traditional Chinese government institutions such as the careful personnel regulations, the collegial organization of various ministries, and the principle of balance maintained by wise emperors. Although the emperors held absolutist power, they could hardly disregard these bureaucratic institutions, time and again reinforced by tradition, without causing great troubles. As unique as the examination system was the censorial system by which appointed officials received petitions, raised complaints, initiated investigations, and even offered criticism as well as advice to the emperor himself. It was fairly effective in checking upon other bureaucrats. While the censors could not impose their opinion upon the emperor, for he alone made the ultimate decision, they were certainly not without some influence under normal circumstances. In comparison, Professor Kracke concludes that by pre-modern Islamic and European standards the individual Chinese citizen under such a government fared rather well. Added to the fact that the Chinese empires were usually of a huge size, it was definitely a remarkable accomplishment.

Perhaps the above selection has put traditional China in a much too favorable light. In any event, it deals mainly with the ideal norms of the central government. When we turn to the realistic situation, we find a different picture. Take the case of local government, for example: we learn from Chapter 8 by Professor Ch'ü, that supervisions were not strict, regulations degenerated into formalities, and corrupt practices became the order of the day. The local magistrate was not alone to blame, many other elements were involved such as his private secretaries, his personal servants, and the clerks who were natives of the area, on the job for a long time, and thoroughly familiar with the local conditions, far more so than he could ever hope to be. Then too, the local gentry or elite families—wealthy and influential—often intervened with pressures that were hard to resist.

Such conditions would in the long run contribute to instability. Striking in Chinese history was the recurrence of dynastic cycle: a dynasty started with good administration and ended through deterioration. In fact no dynasty lasted much longer than three hundred years. Professor Kao in Chapter 9 summarizes why rebellions arose at the end of many dynasties. The usual causes were overpopulation, concentration of land ownership, government taxations, state monopolies, and official corruption. Many uprisings were against the established order; hence, they rallied support by using unorthodox religious beliefs. However, none of them ever triumphed. Unorthodox religious beliefs simply failed to be accepted by the Chinese society at large. On the other hand, a rebellion that did succeed in taking over the whole country and becoming a new dynasty always adopted the same established order with its virtues and without its vices. The self-corrective renovation of the old order is but another illustration, briefly alluded to in Chapter 1, of how tenaciously integrated the traditional Chinese civilization was.

Beginning with Chapter 10, our attention turns to what may be called the "inner dimension" of Chinese civilization. Again, the focus is on integration, not its formalistic elements, such as the uniform written language mentioned in Chapter 1, but its ethico-religious contents. It has been said that the Chinese way of life is humanistic, pragmatic, and realistic. The absence of a creation myth in ancient China and the lack of concern for God as the ultimate source of salvation further separate the Chinese mentality from that of the Judaeo-Christian West. Yet, if the long history of China is a distinctive cultural development as well as a sociopolitical evolution, what are the key values that have shaped the direction of such a development? Are they humanistic, pragmatic, and realistic in the sense of being irreligious, worldly, and unspiritual? Is the Chinese mentality really so foreign to Western consciousness that the twain shall never meet? In the following selections, seven prominent scholars concern themselves with these questions in their analyses of the Chinese Mind.

Professor Derk Bodde in Chapter 10 discusses the interrelation between law (*fa*) and propriety (*li*). His study gives us much insight into the area of social ethics. It is especially interesting to know how the classical demarcation of rule by law and rule by virtue, through centuries of mutual influence, became so thoroughly integrated that the Chinese legal system has to be conceived as the product of interaction between law and propriety, some internal contradictions notwithstanding. Of course, one can easily point to some specific areas where the so-called integration breaks down. Yet, as a whole, it is justifiable to claim that the penetration of ideas into the actual practices of sociopolitical institutions has been greater in traditional China than in the West of the same period. Bodde's article, in this sense, serves a natural bridge between the previous discussions on sociopolitical institutions and the subsequent examination of ethico-religious ideas.

Professor Huston Smith, having extensively studied the great historical religions of men, throws considerable light on the problem of religion in ancient China in Chapter 11. Through his analysis, an important aspect of Chinese "humanism," which has been commonly understood as alien to the humanistic tendency in the West, reveals itself in the midst of many perplexing interpretations. Chapter 12 is a detailed analysis of one of the most important concepts in Chinese philosophy by Professor Wing-tsit Chan. The "history-of-ideas" approach adopted by Professor Chan enables us to see not only the evolutionary development of the concept of *jên,* frequently rendered as human-heartedness, love, benevolence, or humanity, but also the inner dynamism of this Confucian symbol in the Chinese cultural context.

Chapters 13 to 15 include three expositions of the so-called "Three Teachings" (*san-chiao*), referring to Confucianism, Taoism, and Buddhism. The term itself seems to imply the possibility, or at least the wish, of uniting the three in one. The editors recognize that the two selections by Professors T'ang Chün-i (Chapter 13) and Chang Chung-yuan (Chapter 14), in a comparative perspective, seem to require a much more sophisticated level of understanding. Furthermore, their approaches, though greatly appreciated in Taiwan and Hong Kong, are relatively unknown to the West. However, the unique attempts made by them to interpret the religious dimension of Chinese culture are so worth noting that their inclusion, in the view of the editors, is both an appreciation of past efforts and an anticipation of future contributions.

Professor T'ang Chün-i stresses the spiritual values of Confucianism in Chapter 13. It is his contention that man's search for himself is the basis of moral cultivation and human relations in the Confucian tradition. Professor Chang Chung-yuan dwells on the meaning of Tao in Chapter 14. His focus is on the relationship between Tao's creativity and the manifold world. He argues that the Taoist organic concept has greatly influenced both Confucianism and Chinese Buddhism. Chapter 15 is a selection from Professor Kenneth Ch'en's standard study on Buddhism in China. The emphasis is on the Buddhist contributions to Neo-Confucianism and Taoism. In our last selection, Chapter 16, Professor Gernet discusses the religious aspects of Chinese life in the thirteenth century. Through his reconstruction of the historical phenomena, the interpenetration among the "Three Teachings" is vividly presented in the context of popular beliefs.

Professor Wing-tsit Chan has said,

> If one word could characterize the entire history of Chinese philosophy, that word would be humanism—not the humanism that denies or slights a Supreme Power, but one that professes the unity of man and Heaven. In this sense, humanism has dominated Chinese thought from the dawn of its history.

It is in this connection that we believe that the absence of a creation myth or the lack of concern for a personal God does not make the Chinese less involved in the pursuit of ultimate meaning in life. Indeed, he is so much engaged in such a pursuit that his insistence on the importance of here and now, as reflected in Chinese pragmatism and realism, is closely correlated with history on the one hand and religion on the other. If one is really true to oneself here and now, according to his argument, one is simultaneously truthful to one's spiritual as well as biological ancestors and to Heaven (*t'ien*), the most generalized form of universality. Thus the transformation of the self so as to reveal the most sincere self, which is inherent in our nature—sageliness in Confucianism, Buddhahood in Buddhism, or Tao in Taoism—becomes a defining and integrating principle of the Chinese Mind.

The editors are fully aware that the selections included in the present text can only spotlight certain elements of integration in China. The approach of characterizing Chinese civilization by the complex idea of integration certainly demands further investigation, modification, clarification, and reinterpretation. In fact, the very attempt to use integration as a valid concept to describe some features of Chinese civilization is merely one of the many ways of looking at a civilization as long and complex as the Chinese. A proper understanding of this civilization, many of us in the profession firmly believe, can only come about by cooperative efforts of the relevant disciplines through a series of multidimensional evaluations.

1

INTEGRATIVE FACTORS THROUGH CHINESE HISTORY: THEIR INTERACTION

James T. C. Liu

All texts on Chinese history mention its long continuity, a remarkable case in world record, but usually without elaboration, perhaps because many of us would not quite agree on how it should be explained. Recent researches tend to focus more on specific changes than on such generality. Nevertheless, it remains a phenomenon that merits some exchange of opinion from time to time. This review article merely attempts a broad sketch in the hope of inviting further attention and discussion.

To begin with, let us put aside the rather dubious question of dynastic cycle or the rise and fall of respective Chinese empires. For these political events may not have much to do with changes in other phases of the culture. Professor Arthur Wright calls it a regularity generalization, a self-image of Chinese civilization. Professor L. S. Yang, after citing numerous modern works on the divergent causes, raises the question whether many dynastic cycles may have different configurations. My own studies still in progress suggest, for example, that the Northern Sung and the Southern Sung are different, both at their beginnings and at their ends.

Given the complexity of Chinese history, we are generally not very satisfied with single-dimension characterizations: Chinese conservatism, which merely begs the question; general stagnation, which suffers from the same weakness; the theory of hydraulic society, which illuminates one major aspect but leaves so many others unexplained; and the characterization of Chinese history as successive forms of feudal society with some sprouting capitalism in later centuries, which attempts to cut the pieces to make them fit the Marxist jigsaw puzzle. A useful compilation, "The Pattern of Chinese History," edited by Professor John Meskill, summarizes various schemes of periodization, each directing our attention to one kind of crucial change or another. Taken together, they seem to confirm the impression voiced by Professor Charles O. Hucker that Chinese history sounds like an ill-organized orchestration with multiple themes and discordant, even divergent, notes. Still, we can hardly get away from the concept of continuous evolution, not necessarily a linear concept, but a confluence of many interlocking and parallel currents, though, it must be emphasized as with all general discussions, this is not to the exclusion of other views. What Confucius said long ago seems still relevant: "The Yin dynasty followed the rites of Hsia; wherein it took from or added to them may be known. The Chou followed the rites of the Yin; wherein it took from or added to them may be known." To the Chinese mind through the centuries, continuity does not mean "simple succession without change" or *i cheng pu pien*. Rather, it means "succeeding changes" or *yen-ke*, which has an alternate rendering of "both conservatism and reform."

Chinese history, as is true of all history, has to deal with both continuity and change, or stability and adjustment, in fact two sides of the same coin. Conceptually, one may suggest a variety of continual changes such as incremental change, gradual change, renovative change, re-orienting change, cumulative change, drastic change. Or one may see change as through transmission, through transmutation, or through transformation. A vital question would be: What is the relationship between a certain change and the heritage that is actively influential at that particular time? Professor E. A. Kracke, Jr., has described many "changes within tradition" during the Sung. However, others argue that some of these changes were fundamental, irreversible, epoch-making, and decisively beyond the tradition. In fact, it can hardly be overemphasized that the tradition itself is not stagnant. Through selectivity in transmission and reinterpretation in transmutation, the tradition itself evolves. Only because there was neither clear-cut break nor shattering breakdown till the present century, the evolving tradition always claimed to be not only the legitimate heir of the classical tradition, but essentially the very same—though in many respects, as we can clearly discern, not quite the same. Could we not then look upon Chinese history as a complex process of *integration, not just continuity, but through slow continual changes along with modifying and modified tradition?* If this should be acceptable as a basis for exploration, then the question shifts from continuity to integration: How did the Chinese culture and society integrate both changes and tradition? One may see, admittedly at the risk of oversimplification but for the sake of illustration, at least three broad and interacting sets of factors: geographical, intellectual, and institutional. Much of it, though common knowledge, deserves repeating. Many points are synthesized here from the various contributions made by so many well-known scholars in the field that individual citations seem hardly necessary.

China, as is generally known, is geographically isolated. Its huge size, however, should not go unnoticed. The North China plain and its neighboring highlands are larger than other fertile valleys in West and South Asia, where several ancient civilizations arose. Moreover, it was from the very beginning the most productive agricultural area in the ancient world. Moreover, it extends toward the regions to its south without sharp demarcation, as the geographical differences between them are gradual. This facilitated both expansion and integration. Even more significant, China has not just one but *two* broad river valleys, a distinctive advantage no other ancient civilization had. When the first wave of nomadic conquerors took the Yellow River valley, the Han civilization survived in the Yangtze River valley, the Szechuan basin, and other smaller plains in South China—a concrete demonstration of the said advantage. The process of retreat, retrenchment, and further development to new heights often with remarkable changes in the tradition was repeated several times till the Sung. It was not until the Mongols, fairly late in Chinese history, that the entire farming country fell under nomadic conquest. Even if the fleeting notion some Mongols had of reducing North China to pastoral land had been carried out, the other parts would in all probability have carried on. Nor did the Mongol rule last long. One major factor in its downfall was the inability to cope with the complexity of the Yangtze valley. In other words, no other farming civilization had lasted so long against the pressure and intrusions of the so-called "barbarians," who were in many cases highly civilized in their own ways. As a result, the farming heritage was so deep that it could hardly be uprooted. Paradoxically, it was reinforced by many so-called "barbarian" ingredients that came to be accepted and integrated into the overall pattern.

Geography interacted with thought and institutions, mainly the belief in man-made improvement of the land and the organizational ability to carry it out. The two broad river valleys were in time linked by the Grand Canal. Perhaps more important than its tribute traffic was the long-distance regional trade it stimulated. Many lesser streams connected by shorter overland routes also evolved into sprawling networks for regional trade. The military weakness of the Sung on land gave rise to the compensating development of much more river, coastal, and sea shipping. And increasing trade added impetus to regional specialization in manufactured goods and cash crops. Still, China remained largely an agricultural country; the market network permitted cumulative growths but rarely drastic departures. Irrigation was another good illustration. While the central government undertook the large-scale waterworks, it was the local government and private groups that carried out, maintained, and repaired the countless smaller irrigation projects. The knowledge of farming, manufacturing, trading, and irrigation spread more rapidly and more widely when printed books became available, even to many commoners, though for the most part it was the initiative and leadership of local officials and private elite that counted.

Another geographical dimension must be mentioned: the tremendous expansion of agricultural productivity in the last millennium through the coming of new crops, ranging from the early-ripening rice to a variety of plants that made productive the marginal lands, the hillsides, and the sandy lands. Coming directly or indirectly from Southeast Asia and the American continent, they spread gradually from the south to the north, eventually to Manchuria, a new frontier expansion. Significantly, expansion was accompanied by integration, for the new crops usually did not displace the old. Through the tradition of intensive farming, they enriched the variety of cross- and multi-cultivation, characteristic of cumulative development.

There were many products other than food. From ancient times, China was well known for its silk, to wit, the Silk Road across Asia.

Centuries later tea appeared. And about a thousand years ago, cotton came into China and spread rapidly. All these and other cash crops remained largely in the form of household economy among the peasants. In other words, they formed integral parts of agriculture, the mainstay of the national economy.

Certain products lay beyond peasantry or agriculture. The leading examples were chinaware manufacturing, textile industries, and mining. Studies of these industries made in recent years are connected with the problem of incipient capitalism in traditional China. Without going into detail, most scholars would agree that one major reason why capitalism could not develop was the state—its control and intervention in these industries. Such state measures were marked by flexibility, depending on the nature of the case and the particular circumstances. To look at it from the standpoint of the traditional Chinese state itself, it meant the search for integrative supervision—to find a formula that could control the local resources on the one hand and fit well with the state interest on the other.

Greater productivity and a larger volume of trade supported the prosperity of many cities and market towns. Case studies reveal that their growth was on the whole by successive small steps, not by leaps and bounds. However, with their gradual expansion and the spreading of their dense population, the map of China looks like a continuing galaxy of cities, market towns, and villages, with the end of one merging into the beginning of another and the break between them hardly noticeable at all. Many landowners had properties in several neighboring counties, partly a diversification of investment and partly a convenient means of tax evasion. Many city dwellers—elite, merchants, and small storekeepers alike—retained their rural ties. Those who could afford it had multiple residences in the walled city as well as in the countryside. Of great consequence was the radiating diffusion of the urban culture. Well known was the spread of vernacular literature through popular performing arts. Another vivid example was the poor tutor teaching the *Three-character Classics* in a so-called "three household hamlet." The gap between the elitist tradition and the peasant tradition—or what Redfield called the great tradition and the small tradition—in terms of the value system became narrower as time went on. It was this closely knit economic, social, and intellectual web that made it possible for the government of such a vast empire to confine its formal structure mainly in the cities, while utilizing the social structure for rural control. Indeed the geography of China may be seen as more than a galaxy; it becomes a solid block.

Among intellectual factors, the uniform written language bridges across the diverse dialects in both time and space. Another closely connected factor that promoted integration was the strong belief in teachability, by transmission along family lineage, which was made easier through the generations by early marriage, by transforming conquering or immigrating minorities through attrition or contacts, and by aggressive conversion through forcible imposition of the Han culture upon the weak minorities in South, Southwest, and Northwest China.

Underlying this belief in teachability was the ancient view of culture as a cumulative process of successive progress. An outstanding manifestation of this view was the ancient myths: a sequence of legendary cultural heroes, beginning with P'an-ku, followed by fire-inventor, farming inventor, silk inventor, flood-queller, and so on. This outlook of cultural history assumes the beginning of the universe, along with the participation of human efforts. It also assumes an open-end unfolding of the future, always calling for continuous human endeavors. It never postulates an end of the world; as a common saying goes: "If the sky should fall down, there would be all the people to carry it on their shoulders" or *t'ien t'a leh, yu ta-chia kang.* This characteristically Chinese confidence in slow progressive improvement, already expressed earlier by Hsün-tzu and a few other ancient philosophers, seems to be firmly rooted by Han times, as evidenced in the writings of Ssu-ma Ch'ien, the Grand Historian. In spite of the pessimistic mood that arose during the Southern and Northern Dynasties, the confident outlook persisted and revived with greater vigor from the T'ang on. While it had a strong historical-mindedness, to invoke the assumption of an ancient utopia was not really intended to turn the clock back, but essentially to reinforce arguments for corrective measures in the present for the benefit of the future. By the same token, the thrust of neo-Confucianism was by the application of the classical principle toward the search for improvement, often with missionary-like zeal, especially in terms of the expanding cultural integration to include the non-elite. Admittedly, improvements often failed to be realized and good times were hard to come by. However, there was little worry that bad times would last very long; it was always assumed that the process of cultural progress would somehow resume and continue. In this light, Wang Yang-ming's philosophy is most noteworthy. It was in reality an attempt at massive social enlightenment, even when the time was not good at all. It also brought together certain selective elements from both Buddhism and Taoism, an integration of the non-Confucian legacies and an epoch-making achievement that answered the centuries-old call for "the merging of the three teachings" or *san chiao ho i.*

At this point, it seems necessary to mention some characteristics of Confucianism, a vast subject. This is no place to try to classify Confucianism: Is it a religion? a philosophy? a state cult? a way of life? It simply does not fit exclusively in any of these categories. Whatever it is, Confucianism provides a rational or relatively rational approach in understanding as well as in coping with the world. Thereby, it assumes that the world must be an organic whole or an integrated one. Likewise, man's understanding of it must be all-inclusive. This made Confucianism inevitably syncretic. Confronted by the empire system, a legalistic structure, Confucianists accepted the Legalist philosophy to a degree but with a modified interpretation. On supernatural phenomenon, they adopted many elements of the Taoist religion and philosophy. When they realized that Buddhism could not possibly be either uprooted or ignored, they developed neo-Confucianism, a part of which was actually inspired by or derived from Buddhism. In spite of all these adaptations and admixtures, Confucianism never lost its own identity. Above everything else, it persisted as an integrated system that worked for an orderly and humane society.

Buddhism is another vast subject. So powerful and stimulating was its impact upon China that Hu Shih described it as "The Indianization of China." True enough, the Chinese civilization was never the same again. However, the reverse is also true: Buddhism in adapting itself became integrated by the Chinese civilization. For instance, the Chinese Maitreya, the Future Buddha, bears neither resemblance in appearance to its Indian origin nor the same life ideals. In China, it represents wealth, plenty of children, and earthly comfort. Another interesting example is filial piety. Originally absent in Buddhism owing to its monastic discipline and celibacy, it was introduced into Chinese Buddhism, even with the claim that the Buddhist filial piety was superior to all, capable of salvation not only for the soul of one's parents but for all living beings.

In any event, Confucianism through successive readjustment, the acculturized Buddhism, as well as the other intellectual trends of earlier centuries, all became recognized parts of China's heritage.

The reverence for the heritage, the search for improvement, and the urge to integrate them have been embodied in such common mottos as: "inheriting the past, while opening up the future" or *chi wang k'ai lai,* as well as in what may be called the genre of *t'ung* or comprehensive work: such as the three great encyclopedias known as the *T'ung chih, T'ung k'ao,* and *T'ung tien;* also the monumental chronicle entitled *Tzu-chih t'ung-chien* or "Comprehensive mirror for aid in government." A large number of provincial gazetteers likewise go by the title of *t'ung-chih* or comprehensive record. The usage extends to vernacular publications: for example, calendars known as *t'ung-li.* Another example is the genre of popular historical tales known as *t'ung-su yen-i,* in which *t'ung* means comprehensive and *su* means popular or vulgar. Another connotation of *t'ung* in verbal form means to understand comprehensively. The common saying "*po ku t'ung chin*" means "having a wide knowledge of the past as well as a comprehensive understanding of the present." The concept of *t'ung* clearly implies a conviction: to call upon the past as a reference in order to insure a balance in the needed improvement and changes of the present and the future. The same spirit prevailed, for example, in the development of paintings. Early masterpieces were respected, studied, and copied, yet innovations appeared from time to time. The stylistic morphology usually stayed within the tradition but sometimes developed beyond its confines, though without openly or completely breaking away from it.

Among institutional factors, what readily comes to mind is the centralized form of government. Several multi-states in ancient Chou had been moving in that direction through several centuries. The Ch'in, the first unified empire, was the cumulative outcome. Since then, China chose to stay with this system almost without interruption, again a rare phenomenon in world history. Even during the weakness of the central power, during the periods of division, and among the ephemeral regimes that were much reduced in territorial size or in actual control, the same pattern of government continued, reflecting the persistent urge to integrate, or at least the hope of being able to do so. It did not mean that the faults of this system went unnoticed. As late as the seventeenth century, leading intellectuals reopened the question whether some form of enfeoffment or separate domains under loose overall control would not work better than the oversized and unwieldy centralized form. However, both conventional theories and historical experience indicated that such arrangements would result in friction, conflict, and disintegration. For unification and integration, no viable alternative to centralized empire seemed to be available.

Political integration did not depend on centralization alone. Much reliance was placed in the last millennium on a homogeneous class of scholar-officials. Despite all kinds of trouble among them, especially factionalism and excessive power held by imperial favorites, the scholar-officials were generally held together by a common educational background and value system. Integration of the bureaucracy went one step further after the Sung with the establishment of a firm civilian superiority over the military. The stabilizing effect of this can hardly be exaggerated. Between the first Sung emperor and Yüan Shik-k'ai, no usurpation by any official, apart from royal princes and rebel leaders, ever succeeded. An integration so achieved had to pay a heavy price. One penalty was the increasing aggravation of autocratic tendencies. Another disadvantage was persistent conservatism throughout the administration. To cope with the many baffling problems, it always seemed safer to coast along the established ways, to fulfill the formalities, and to make only minor adjustments. This conservative approach did not exactly spell stagnation. The administrative system under the Ming and the Ch'ing was far more refined than that of the Sung. Refinement means inward improvement and even stronger integration that was able to resolve conflicts and contain tensions.

This institutional development went hand in hand with the intellectual atmosphere. The search for improvement, as mentioned a while ago, precluded radical departures on the ground that they carried the risk of much disruption. Even those late-century scholars who admired Wang An-shih expressed the regret that his reform attempted too much and went too far. In contrast, the single-whip system of taxation—a change of great magnitude during the Ming—represented a successful example of relatively smooth transformation. Introduced pragmatically and extended gradually, it did not entail much change in related government functions. The slow, cautious, and piecemeal style of change was regarded as the best means for the system to correct and reinforce itself. Even more conservative in consequence was the concept of "social role" or *wei jen*. It implies conformity: one should fit himself into the role required by the institutional framework.

Another striking feature of Chinese history is the lack of successful revolution. For example, how did the aristocrats up to the T'ang period come to be replaced. Slowly weakened by a variety of factors over more than a century of chaotic times, they faded away, but not without leaving many of their descendants to compete and to mingle with the emerging class of nonhereditary scholar-officials, who on their part also took over through transmutation and integration much of the artistocratic heritage. There was similarly an apparent lack of class consciousness in peasant rebellions. They rebelled against the regime, but not against the system of government as such. They turned against abusive officials and oppressive landowners, but they did not declare war on the bureaucratic landowning class as a whole. Dynasties came and went, but generally the same kind of ruling class survived and revived. Many bureaucrats and would-be bureaucrats offered their service to a new winner. He who had started as the leader of a peasant rebellion became the founding emperor and accepted their service. Whom else could he turn to for the expert management of the vast and complex empire? There was neither a comparable nor competitive group available.

Political integration after all is not as basic as social integration. We may look at the ruling class from another angle. From the end of the Han through the period of disunity, the *hoa tsu* or powerful aristocratic clans tended to be disintegrative forces, politically speaking, from the standpoint of the central government. On the other hand, it may be argued that they, together with the dependent groups under their control, represented regional clusters of continuity and integration. Moreover, what is not so well known was the crucial historical crisis the social structure went through during this period. Between the late third century and the early fourth century, many intellectuals in high society became so disillusioned with the established ways that they dressed strangely, experimented with drugs, explored new religious and philosophical ideas, indulged in unconventional behavior, and even had mixed parties, unheard of in any other period of Chinese history. Sociologically, the family relationships were weakened and individual options were on the rise. The probability was rather strong that at this point Confucian China might well turn into a neo-Taoist China; if so, the historical development would have been entirely different. What reversed the trend? First, the common people retained their family organization as before for economic subsistence as well as for group self-protection in times of unsettling conditions. Second, with the coming of the non-Han peoples into North China, both high and low class had two alternatives: to flee or to defend themselves by fortification. Either case required a well-knit organization. And the family and clan ties furnished the natural answers. Third, the same political disaster was a shock that led to reflection. Most intellectuals retreated from neo-Taoism and returned to the fold of Confucianism, at least its emphasis on family, clan, and community relations. From then on, even after the disappearance of *hao-tsu* or powerful clans after the T'ang period, such emphasis never received any serious challenge.

To analyze further, what is the leading attribute of the Chinese kinship system? One theory holds that the father-son relationship is the dominant one. It implies both continuity and integration. The chain of continuity is obvious: the father leads the son, the son will in turn become a father, and the paternal lineage goes on. Around this core the other members of the family are integrated and the integration is further reinforced by the father's authority. It is almost in direct contrast, for example, to the modern Western society where the dominant kinship relationship is that of husband and wife. The husband-wife relationship is not necessarily continuous, as one of them may pass away or they may be separated. Nor is it integrative: the grown-up son has his own spouse. By nature, the husband-wife relationship is exclusive and nonextendable.

From Sung times on, under the new ruling class of landowning scholar-officials, the Chinese society became increasingly solidified. It was more integrated than ever before. Neither the Mongol rule, nor its downfall, nor the disastrous upheavals at the end of the Ming, nor the Manchu conquest caused much social change. Many factors entered into this long stability of roughly ten centuries. The nonhereditary nature of the ruling class, the fact that many leading families did not remain prominent after a few generations, and the open gate of upward social mobility which was not limited to the ladder of success in civil service examination but also existed in trade for example, offered a hope to many people: those on the fringe of the ruling class and others who wished that their sons might have a chance of joining it. It was a hope that drew the non-elite mass much closer to the elite. The geographical intermingling of the non-elite and the elite through the urban-rural continuum, as mentioned earlier, helped in the same direction. Above all, the most important development was the intricate strengthening of the social web: to wit, the growth of many kinds of social organizations. Many clan or *tsu* maintained ancestral halls, common cemeteries, charitable estates, charitable granaries, and clan schools. Various trades and crafts had their guilds. People from a particular region specializing in a particular trade formed their own groups in distant parts of the country. Officials, degree candidates, merchants, and traders from the same native place gathered together in their own *landsmannschaften* or *hui-kuan* in various large cities. Besides, there were local gangs, smuggling rings, and secret societies. This great variety of social organizations by no means tells the whole story. As one person usually belonged to more than one of these groups or had a close personal bond with another person who belonged to some other organization, these social organizations were in effect interlocked. In addition to the interlocking web, there was the well-known collusion among the officials, their private secretaries, the merchants, the local government clerks, their respective relatives and friends.

Because the entire society was so closely integrated through the interlocking of so many groups and links, personal connection was held at a premium. For someone away from home to find his way in this amazingly intricate maze he had to search for social ties. Hence, the social convention of translating the social ties into personalized terms under the concept of "common identity" or "common root" called *t'ung*. The term *t'ung* was applied most extensively. People of the same surname but from different regions and completely unrelated claimed to be *t'ung-tsung* or common descendants of an assumed ancestry. Those whose names were Liu, Kuan, Chang, Chao, just because of the four famous sworn brothers in the "Romance of the Three Kingdoms," claimed they were still so related. People from neighboring provinces claimed to be "extended fellow natives" or *ta t'ung-hsiang,* as distinct from the ordinary *t'ung-hsiang* or fellow natives of the same province and the closer kind of *hsiao-t'ung-hsiang,* those from the same county. Those who earned their degrees at examinations in different provinces but in the same year considered themselves to be *t'ung-nien* or class of the same year. Once being colleagues or *t'ung-shih,* the relationship was always recognized thereafter. Those who found one another's scholarly, philosophical, or religious inclinations more or less similar considered themselves "fellow travellers" or *t'ung-tao.* Those who shared the same hobby were known as "fellow players" or *t'ung-hao* (*hao* of fourth tone). Even in Republican days, fellow citizens are called *t'ung-p'ao,* that is, brothers and sisters from the same womb or motherhood. The concept of *t'ung* implies identity and, for the society as a whole, integration. More than a mere social convention, people were aware or being made aware of its permeating implication.

Integration is never complete. Within a culture, there are always internal disparities, incongruities, tensions, and conflicts. Nor is integration a constant; the degree of cohesiveness varies in time and under varying circumstances. Nonetheless, a closely knit society such as traditional China seems to have generated through the centuries a momentum to build up an ever-multiplying variety of social ties in the hope of resolving conflicts and containing tensions. Within the matrix formed by all these warps and woofs, it seems that no force—social, political, or economic—could possibly emerge from within that society itself to cause radical changes, let alone to tear apart the integration so formed over many centuries. The only force capable of causing a disintegration had to come from the outside: an overpowering assault that brought drastic changes in the economy and economic geography, an intellectual revolution, and an institutional breakdown. Even then, the process of disintegration took at least half a century. Perhaps it has to go on for some time yet, as the gigantic task of modern reintegration remains today a most absorbing problem.

2

GENERAL CHARACTERISTICS OF CHINESE GEOGRAPHY

Joseph E. Spencer

THE QUALITIES OF THE ENVIRONMENT

The physical landscape of China today is rather different from that existing six or seven thousand years ago. The beautiful mosaic patterns of terraced fields did not exist, and the thousand of miles of dikes had not been built. Forests of several kinds covered much more of the country than is true today, and soil erosion had not dug its destructive fingers into many parts of China to lessen the value of the land to a farming people. It seems a fair statement that no other landscape in the world has had such a percentage of its surface made over by man, purposefully or because of him. As previously described the landscape of China is a checkerboard pattern of mountain strips and lowland plains and basins. The lowlands are scattered widely, and the dissected hill and mountain landscapes comprise by far the greater portion of the area of China. In soils, vegetation, and climate there is a tremendous variety from northern Manchuria to Hainan Island. After several thousand years of living in parts of the landscape the landscape today shows that the Chinese have made the most of its variety while at the same time planting certain common cultural traits everywhere. However, it certainly must have been possible, let us say, at 2700 B.C. to pick out several clear types of local environments, separated not by linear

From *Asia, East by South* by Joseph E. Spencer (New York: John Wiley & Sons, Inc., 1954), pp. 300–304, 306–10. Reprinted by permission of the publisher.

boundaries but merging through transition zones. Though this environmental complex is not able to support the present enormous population of China, it was more than adequate for any demands upon it in the earliest periods.

The area that was covered by loess and alluvial deposits, the Loess Highlands and the North China Plain, certainly must have comprised a unique region of North China. It probably was an open landscape without a heavy or difficult vegetation cover, with soils that were easily worked by simple means and that were rich enough to yield good returns under casual treatment. The hard-rock highlands projecting above the loess and alluvial cover probably never lost all their forest cover. The soft loess lands certainly were without widespread surface water supplies, but the scattered highlands, and their margins, must have had better water supplies all during the loessial period. The main streams throughout the area must have carried a seasonably variable volume of water. Climatically this whole region had a long, cold winter with much dust and wind, and a medium-length hot summer with low, variable precipitation. The precipitation total may have been a little greater than at present. If its winter dust and low temperatures and its precarious summer precipitation make it seem less attractive today than our modern conception of a Garden of Eden, it did have the very real advantages of rich soil, rock, wood, and water all relatively near at hand everywhere, with a wide variety of grains, fruits, and animals to choose from. Early man asked less of his environment than do we today. All these resources were present in an area of North China large enough to permit a scattering of several local centers or groups of tribes who did not, in the beginning, have to fight for possession of a single small prize area. The corridor along the northern footslope of the Tibetan Plateau afforded a passable connection to all of central Asia and constituted, from the very beginning, an important feature of the North China environment.

It is hard to suggest the regional limits of the open loess and alluvial landscape. To the northwest, however, it must have faded off into the more arid and monotonous landscapes of the Mongolian Plateau country. Here the shallow, open basins, with seasonal flood lakes or dry sandy and salty floors, alternated with the grass-covered aprons, basin margins, and rocky drainage divides. The better-situated spots were usable grasslands; the poorer localities were barren rock flats or desert strips from which the loess had been removed. No sharp line separated these two landscape types, but rather a broad and gradual transition. The structural elements of the Chinese checkerboard do not accord with the distribution of precipitation in this part of China. The lines of the Yin Shan and the Ala Shan lie well out in the grasslands and in no sense formed a significant environmental boundary. Farther and farther out in the grasslands the volume of easily exploited environmental resources became more and more limited, and this open grassland presented a poorer environment than that of the loess and alluvial landscape nearer the coast.

Southward from loessland there was a sharper change of another variety. Particularly in the west of China the high Tsinling Shan system sets a barrier across the land. The north and south sides of the Tsinling present one of the strongest and sharpest zones of contrast in all China. Eastward as the Tsinling Shan steadily lowers and becomes less formidable the contrast becomes less sharp and more of a transition, but the facts of contrast have been there at all times. This southern landscape was a subtropical environment, moist and rainy much of the year, with an all-year growing season, and with vegetation in the form of forests covering all except the floodplains. Bamboo, the citrus fruits, palms and a host of other trees, shrubs, and flowering plants were present. The water buffalo, rhinoceros, elephants, monkeys, and other tropical birds and animals replaced the fauna of North China. Here, less effort was needed to secure a fair existence in a mild environment, but the very lack of a natural nucleus probably prevented human concentration upon a particular region.

Other minor contrasts might be mentioned. The litoral of the coastal fringe, from southern Korea around to the southern coast of Chekiang, Shantung and Liaotung excepted, presented a marshy, muddy fringe of saline soils, high water table, and tall grass and reeds that was less usable than the higher, drier parts of the alluvial fill. A part of the Yangtze floodplain undoubtedly shared this same water-logged nature. Even today the Chinese only partially have mastered the appropriate uses for this kind of landscape, and in the earlier periods it was not a sought-after section of China. Similarly, northward into Manchuria where neither loess nor alluvial fill provided soft and easily tilled land, the shorter growing season, the colder snowy winter, and the heavier forest cover combined to frame an environment that has attracted the Chinese only within the present century.

THE PEOPLES AND CULTURES OF FOLK HISTORY

The discovery of Peking Man and his contemporaries seems to indicate that perhaps the same types of people have lived in China throughout much of human history, but it proves nothing with regard to the origin of the body of culture now labeled Chinese. And the continued presence in this part of eastern Asia of related physical types does not preclude repeated migration and counter-migration across, into, and out of the separate local environments within the major region. It is quite impossible today to place the specific regional home of the Mongoloid races and, similarly, it is almost impossible to place the exact region in which the Chinese type of Mongoloid man first developed. From numerous bits of evidence much of Chinese folk history appears truly to point to migrations within eastern Asia and to long-continued residence in North China.

With respect to material culture, the earliest folk history indicated interest in problems of water control, in flood, drought, and irrigation. It relates the beginnings of agriculture, mainly concerned with the evolution of cultivation and crop handling. However, this folk history suggests that animals had a place in folk economy, and that there also was a place for fishing operations. It was concerned with several rather unique items, among them being silk and jade. It showed an awareness that in other geographical regions there were other ways of supporting existence. Metals and the fabrication of various implements are parts of the pattern but do not dominate it.

Beyond the material aspects of culture in this Chinese folk history the manner of dealing with human relationships was somewhat different from that of other folk histories. Calculations regarding the seasonal and calendar cycles became tied up with divination of floods, droughts, and other supernatural troubles, and rites propitiating the gods became intertwined with ceremonies honoring the ancestors. There accumulated a mass of folk culture rather unlike that accumulating in other parts of Eurasia, and with it came a peculiar awareness of the differences between this culture and those about it.

The specific statements of Chinese folk history are as impossible of application in a literal sense as the doings of the divine beings of Greek mythology or the accounts of the earlier eras among the American Sioux. But since 1930 a critical pursuit of archaeology and history has gradually pieced together a long and complicated story that promises to outdo the folk history not only in complication but in duration of time and sheer variety of performance. Only a start has been made in unraveling the Stone Age geography of China, and no critical judgment so far can be set upon the period. Chinese culture seems to be not as old as that of India and the Near East. Many of the fundamental inventions came in from the Indian-Near Eastern realm, but numerous features were acquired from southeastern Asia. It may well be that agriculture itself, as a technique, came from some other part of Asia, transmitted along the central Asian corridor. But under these additions is a basic body of Chinese culture, formulated in an early North China hearth, that even today is fundamental to an understanding of China.

THE PRIMARY CULTURE OF THE NORTH CHINA HEARTH

Good soils, water, wood, stone, and domesticable plants and animals in abundance all lay close at hand in the landscape of the Chinese culture hearth in the Huang River Basin. There certainly were variations in the region, and numerous local, superior sites were separated from each other in space and situation. The total central area of such landscapes is in the vicinity of 200,000 square miles. After the close of the glacial era, as loess deposition and alluvial sedimentation slowed down, this region would seem to have been the most attractive part of eastern Asia to groups of people just learning to handle the simplest problems of rudimentary agriculture and animal husbandry, settlement formation, and society organization. And if it was a superior environment it also was a malleable one which could reasonably be changed and shaped to fit the early group decisions and organizational politics of the peoples who permanently occupied it. This simple flexibility was, so to speak, an essential virtue of a hearth environment for any culture group just entering its formative stage and not yet crystallized into specific modes of operating a landscape or an economy.

Though this open landscape covered a large territory it graded off into other kinds of landscapes in all directions. Along these marginal transitions, in the earliest eras, there was no conclusive environmental stimulus in one direction only. It is only in more recent periods of culture history that we can begin, even, to draw sharp boundary zones between distinctive landscapes, after a long process of selective human use and development has accented certain features of the environment. Once development started, the pertinent natural resources gave the primitive economy an advantage over that of surrounding territories. Every forward step slowly increased that advantage to make this an outstanding region. Even under primitive conditions its population density must have exceeded that of neighboring regions, a fact which further favored the hearth area. In this central North China hearth there was organized an agriculture that drew upon many native plants, such fruits as the apricot, peach, plum, persimmon, and pear, such plants as several millets and buckwheat, and that early adapted plants and animals from other domestication centers. In addition there were forest-borne nuts and many wild animals available for the hunting. The irregular rainfall and the presence of streams in the alluvial lands fostered an awareness and a promotion of primitive irrigation once agriculture was understood. Already the initial step had been taken in settling up an intensive agriculture. The differences between portions of the hearth were slight and unimportant compared to the larger contrasts between the hearth and the grasslands or the subtropical southern forest.

Material culture was not only the product of the hearth. Inevitably certain culture traits were fostered in this homeland unlike those developed in outside, unlike environments. As the sedentary hearth developed there followed the universal tendency to look down upon those who did not practice the same customs. Gradually and somewhat unconsciously the hearth population came to think of themselves as "we, the cultured" and of all peoples of the transitions, margins, and lands beyond as uncultured barbarians. This is a common human tendency, but Chinese culture eventually developed this feeling into a very strong self-centeredness.

THE CULTURES OF THE BARBARIAN FRINGE

The self-centeredness of the North China hearth has a very real basis. On the Mongolian grasslands the mature pastoral economy that characterized Ghengis Khan's time had not yet evolved. The economic opportunities of the grasslands in the third millennium before Christ cannot have been great, even though repeated overgrazing had not yet worn them down. Then its contrast to the loesslands was less than it now is, but its resources permitted no great development without an integrated social organization. The simple pastoral economy of the grassland transition was in contrast to the sedentary agriculture of the North China hearth. The precarious environment constantly produced human surpluses which flowed toward the hearth in a steady movement that is one of the most marked features of the history of eastern Asia. The process, certainly was at work by the end of the Neolithic period, has operated throughout recorded Chinese history.

Northeastward short summers and cold winters combined with an irregular forest cover in pointing inhabitants toward some variety of hunting-fishing-gathering-pastoral economy. The Korean section and the southern, unforested, portion of the Manchurian lowland eventually became a Chinese colonial fringe, but in the earliest periods no regional economy here could compare with the pattern of the open lands farther south.

Southward in the Yangtze Valley a watery lowland landscape made reeds, boats, stilt houses, and aquatic food of greater human significance than in North China. Here human inventiveness was being exercised upon the innumerable potentialities of such plants as the bamboo. A marginal sprinkling of Negrito peoples in the coastal lowlands of South China, and a backwash of proto-Malay seafaring folk along the whole South China littoral, gave the coastal fringe a racial variety not found inland and pointed up the use of tropical items in the environment. South China was a big country, with much local variety, a hilly landscape with many local basins and a long and irregular coastline. There were many slight variations in its earliest sprinkling of population. A number of locally favored regions became minor culture centers. Most of them used the common materials of the subtropical environment, but there was no outstanding hearth, and none that rivaled the North China hearth. . . .

THE ECONOMIC PHILOSOPHY OF HAN SOCIETY

The Chinese culture hearth had developed as an intensive agrarian society operated by villages administered by regional city centers. Only a simple range of implements, tools, and mechanical agents were available. Self-sufficiency was not complete, but only a relatively small volume of trade was needed and commercialism was a minor aspect of hearth culture. The end of feudalism required time; practical methods of land ownership and the adjustment and shifting of taxation from crops to land and to the individual owners could not be devised overnight. Chinese hearth society had not developed a large slave labor force as did Greece and Rome, but corvee labor was exacted by the state to accomplish its public works projects. Convicts and "political criminals" also were used on public works. The last century of feudal time and the whole of Han times were a period in which the economic principles of operating an agrarian society were strongly debated. A few revolutionary reformers were rejected, and Chinese economy remained true to its older patterns. Confucian scholars divided into schools of thought over taxation principles, land tenure, the place of trade and handicrafts, and the admissible degree of state participation in agriculture and handicrafts. Some of the discussions read almost word for word like current debates about the economic philosophy of American society.

In spite of the best intentions of government a landlord class arose, along with a segment of the population who became landless tenants. Similarly, a small though prosperous merchant class developed and maintained itself. The scholar-bureaucrats did very well by themselves economically. Han times were a period of settling into accepted molds and patterns of conduct, and of rejecting patterns that involved too great change from the past. Various ills of the state were adjusted, or corrected, or manipulated as they arose. There had been no real precedents to go on, though all adherents to a cause drew such justifications from the Confucian classics as could be found. Though there unquestionably were maladjustments in the patterns of society that crystallized by the end of the Han, the system worked reasonably well for all concerned. Successful molds had been poured for a regionally self-contained agrarian society that operated intensively with a minimum of equipment and a minimum of commerce and handicraft industry.

Modern comparative study of mechanized American agriculture proves that intensive oriental agriculture produces somewhat more actual food per acre than does the American system. However, the man-days of labor involved are far greater in oriental agriculture and the present volume of food production per capita in the Orient is far below that of contemporary United States. However, during Han times it is significant that the intensive system was an improvement over any other economy then operative in eastern Asia and led to a dominance by the Chinese hearth area. The spread of this intensive system was a part of the spread of Chinese culture. It was supervised by a centrally pyramided but very loosely articulated professional bureaucracy with a definite stake in the over-all success of the system. The system involved drawing enough food, manpower, and materials from the empire at large by imperial authority to properly maintain the hearth's political power, to maintain the military power to defend the empire from aggression, and to keep the system in operation.

SETTLEMENT MORPHOLOGY

From an incomplete study of the subject it would appear that at a very early time the inhabitants of the culture hearth came to prefer two definite settlement forms, the compact village and the centrally located city. Dwelling in fixed settlements was one of the fundamental features distinguishing Chinese culture.

The Chinese village is always a compact affair, though it may have various shapes. Houses are built tightly against one another, and there seldom are spacious yards and gardens as in the American small town or hamlet. The most common shape is the shoestring village, a double row of houses along a single street. The site often is a dike top or a stream terrace or bench. Sometimes among the larger trade villages is found the rough grid pattern with one or two streets dominating, and now and then irregular and odd-shaped villages occur. The village varies in size from perhaps a dozen buildings to a thousand houses, with about a hundred houses seeming to be a fair average. Common to all Chinese villages are tea shops, restaurants, inns, and a temple, plus the itinerant goods peddler. Only large villages have grain, cloth, metal, furniture, and other shops. Almost all shops double as private homes, and there seldom is zoning of functions in a village. In north China villages normally are walled, but elsewhere in China it is uncommon to find many walled villages. . . .

In architectural features Chinese settlements show an amazing diversity while at the same time exhibiting a striking superficial similarity. Adobe brick is the commonest building material all over China, but many regional special forms are found. Roofs normally are of gray tile or of straw thatch. North China seldom spruces up its buildings, but west and south China frequently uses whitewash and decorative designs. Domestic architecture in China always has been plain and simple, but public architecture has had a flair for the ornate, elaborate, and highly decorated. The curved roof popularly associated with China is a feature chiefly of public building that has been developed in recent centuries, though some homes of the wealthy families also show it. Out of the culture hearth of North China came the basic features of Chinese building, which have spread wherever the Chinese have gone. These features are the rectangular room unit with few doors and windows. The roof is normally supported on a skeleton of wooden poles independent of the walls which normally are panels filling in the spaces. The room unit can be multiplied any number of times, arranged in L, U, or closed square shapes, the whole set upon a terrace foundation to get it above ground level. In compact settlements various modifications of the rectangular room are found. Most Chinese building is single storied in villages and single or double storied in cities. Only special public buildings and monuments normally reach more than two stories, so that the average Chinese settlement shows a flat skyline unlike that of the large occidental city. In their spread over China, however, the Chinese have taken on many extraneous building materials and housetypes, which actually provide, today, a widely varied architecture. The flat mud-roofed houses of the northwest of China contrast with the steel and concrete skyscraper of the port cities of the China coast, to suggest only two of the many.

THE EXPANDING COLONIAL FRONTIER

Following upon the Han military conquest of the neighboring regions was the process of implanting Chinese culture in the conquered areas. The devices that had accompanied the transformation of feudal China into imperial China worked with considerable satisfaction. The *hsien* or county, the *chün* or military corps area, and the *chou* or political district were the principal administrative regional units that were set up over the new territory. Each was subject to change according to conditions of the specific region. The *chün* was at first less a region of so many square miles than a route between the hearth and some outlying district. Eventually the *sheng* or province matured out of a variety of major political regions of control. Along with the regional devices went the walled city as the functional heart of each new region incorporated into the political administration. The walled city became an advance outpost in an alien landscape and culture. The walled city offered security in times of stress, but infiltration of the countryside was carried out in peaceful periods. The village became the normal rural unit in advance of the city, but not everywhere was it used. In Szechwan Chinese penetration had actually preceded the end of feudal times, and, here, with the walled city as a primary protective control, settlement spread out first over the Chengtu Plain and then the rest of the Szechwan Basin in the form of scattered homesteads.

Where there were barbarian peoples occupying the areas of colonization they were dealt with in various ways. In some areas forced transplantation was used, whereas in others continued residence eventually produced assimilation into the Chinese blood and culture complex. Some of the barbarian groups kept shifting southward ahead of Chinese colonization, themselves pushing still others in a slow drift southward into southeastern Asia. Regardless of what precise method of disposal was used, the Chinese were dominant in culture, administrative control, and numbers. Commencing with the best local centers and those most easily built into bases of operation, the slow process of Chinese colonization of the southland began to fill in the regions bypassed in the earlier military conquest. It was to be a long process, and one not yet complete at the present time. In Fukien the remainders of alien peoples and cultures today are but vestigial remnants. Hainan Island, Kweichow, and Yunnan, on the other hand, are regions in which the Chinese no more than equal the so-called "non-Chinese" at the present time. They have pushed these modern "barbarians" off the best lands, monopolized the political, economic, and social administration of the territory, and extended their lines of influence completely throughout the region. The "non-Chinese" have given the Chinese many things and have absorbed much of Chinese culture, but many of them persistently hang onto language, dress, ceremonial customs, and other marks of their own cultures. Along the Tibetan frontier the Chinese colonization stalled somewhat against the rough and rugged landscape not easily amenable to sedentary, agricultural settlement, and there are blocks of territory occupied by "barbarian" peoples over whom the Chinese even today possess only nominal control or influence.

On the north and west Chinese culture found landscapes not so amenable to the techniques of colonization used in the south. Out into Inner Mongolia, away from the old hearth and into the grasslands, the Chinese repeatedly have pushed. In wet cycles and periods of strong Chinese power they have advanced their lines, only to blow away in the "dust bowl" episodes of dry cycles, and to shrink back under nomad raids in periods of inadequate Chinese strength. Along the central Asian corridor the standard Chinese technique of making Chinese of all other peoples did not work well either, since the Chinese themselves were always a minimum element in the population totals. Repeated efforts in Sinkiang over the centuries have to date achieved only bitterness, unrest, and internal distress, as alien cultures have held strong against Chinese political and military pressure. Northward into Manchuria the Chinese, in this century, have swarmed in such numbers as to sweep all before them in the southern and central lowlands. The northern fringe and the hill strips on either border are not yet colonized. Though their political control has been, and still remains, shaky, Manchuria is Chinese in blood, culture, and economics. The process of Chinese colonization and frontier expansion is not complete on any modern frontier of China, and there is no indication that activity has ceased. . . .

CHINESE ACCULTURATION THROUGH EXPANSION

The earliest expansion out of the hearth found the Chinese firmly convinced that they were superior to any and all barbarian folk of the marginal landscapes. This self-centeredness did not prevent Chinese assimilation of many barbarian customs, in a rather selective manner. Pastoral folk assimilated into Chinese culture brought relatively little; they never did cause the Chinese to take up the use of dairy products. South of the Tsinling the process was relatively more complete but still selective. Bamboo, rice, and the water buffalo were not parts of the original ancient hearth culture, but they are intrinsic parts of modern China wherever climatically practical. The elephant, however, was apparently not liked by the Chinese as a domestic animal, though as an art form it is very common in many parts of China. These are but random examples of the process.

Chinese who went beyond their own borders, as the pilgrims to India, as the traders to the Indies, or as the diplomatic emissaries to tributary kingly courts, brought many things back to China not only of religion and the world of ideas but also of art, architecture, plants, tools, and methods of artisanry. Tribute missions to the Chinese court always brought the special products of their own home environments. The Chinese have taken these things into their culture and transformed them variably to their own ends. Not a century was without some new features; scarcely a generation did not witness the gradual increase in the ideas and the materials that made up Chinese culture. Naturally there were peak periods and low periods in this acquisitional process. The several centuries of the Han, the time of Sui and T'ang, the Mongol Yuan dynasty, the early Ch'ing dynasty, and the last century have been, possibly, the peak eras of cultural expansion.

But in all this contact the Chinese never have lost control over the process of acculturation. Though the process seems largely to have been an unconscious one, strong reaction has always set in against any feature that threatened the fundamental balance of Chinese culture. Never was the firm stable nucleus of the classical China of the North China culture hearth ever basically altered. . . .

3

ECONOMIC AND SOCIAL CHANGES IN T'ANG AND SUNG CHINA

Denis C. Twitchett

During the late T'ang and the Five Dynasties period there seems to have been a sharp increase in the employment of personal dependants of a semi-servile status, especially among the military officials of the new provinces. Such personalized relationships took many forms, for instance the highly intimate form of fictitious adoption, through which personal dependence was strengthened by the addition of "parental discipline," but by far the most widespread and influential of these new relationships was the new status-relationship between landlord and tenants.

In the tenth and eleventh centuries, the tenant farmers (*tien-hu*) came to form a distinct personal status-category, with severe legal restrictions upon their personal liberty. This problem has been the major preoccupation . . . in the formulation of the theory, widely accepted in Japanese Marxist historical circles, that the period from about A.D. 800–1000 saw the transition of Chinese society from the stage of "slavery" to that of "feudalism" or "medieval serfdom."

The chief argument for this has been the indisputable fact that the tenancy system in force upon many Sung estates presents some suggestive parallels with medieval villeinage. The tenant under the new system was not only obliged to pay rent, usually in the form

From *Land Tenure and Social Order in T'ang and Sung China* by Denis C. Twitchett (New York: Oxford University Press, 1962), pp. 28–32. Excerpted by permission of the author. Original footnotes have been deleted.

of a fixed share of the crop, to his landlord, as his T'ang predecessor had been, he also had to perform various labour dues, to render many customary gifts over and above the fixed rent, and to pay a sort of amercement before the marriage of his children. Most important of all, the "tenant" was prohibited from leaving the land which he cultivated, and if his landlord sold this land the "tenant" passed to the new owner as an integral part of the property.

We need not take too seriously the few hotheads who have proclaimed that here we have feudalism in full force rearing its ugly head, and that here begins that "feudalism" which continued to characterize Chinese rural society down until 1840 or even until 1949. This argument does not hold water for a moment, since the highly restrictive tenancy contracts I have mentioned disappear in the early Ming, when a further major revolution in land tenure occurred. But the fact remains that in southern and south-eastern China, the area where during the Southern Sung the system of great estates was most densely developed, many of the cultivators were in a position of legal subservience to their landlords, and even when the legal restrictions upon their freedom were removed during the Ming, they remained in very many cases in a position of economic dependence which continued to restrict severely their freedom of action. . . .

The Sung system of tenancy, however, was not universal. A high proportion of independent free peasants—probably in excess of 60 per cent of the total population—remained. Moreover, it was not simply a one-sided system of exploitation of the peasantry. Many small farmers voluntarily became tenants because a powerful and rich landlord could shield them from the attentions of the tax-gatherers and also because the large *chuang-yüan*[1] as an economic unit offered security and stability, and the possibility of surviving hard times, which were impossible for a small man farming on his own account at bare subsistence level.

Moreover, the "tenants" themselves did not form a homogeneous group. . . . Many tenants continued to work land of their own side by side with the lands rented from their landlord, and there were an infinite number of fine shadings of social status between

[1] [Large land estate, considered by some scholars as somewhat comparable to European manors.]

the free farmer who paid rent to work a piece of land belonging to a neighbouring landlord on the one hand, and the virtual serf without any personal possessions living in a settlement owned by the landlord and using the landlord's implements on the other.

It was, in addition, to the landlord's own advantage not to treat his "tenants" too harshly, and the family rules compiled in Sung times usually advise the family members on this subject. A body of loyal tenants was not merely a labour force used to provide the family income. In periods of unrest it also afforded protection both against bandits and against the subaltern officers of the local *yamen,* who frequently attempted to levy illegal impositions. In many cases we read of tenants being provided with weapons for this purpose.

Nevertheless, it was as a labour force that the "tenants" were primarily recruited, and it was as an economic unit that the *chuang-yüan* was managed. Already in the pre-T'ang period the monastic communities, who had great numbers of dependent families of a semi-servile status, had been able to use this large labour force, backed by their great reserves of wealth, in clearing and breaking in new lands for cultivation, in particular building up great estates from wooded hill-land which could hardly have been effectively cleared by single families of simple peasants. In the same way Sung landlords played a very large role in the reclamation of farm lands from river-bottoms, lake-beds, swamps, sandbanks and coastal flats. Reclamation works on the largest scale were mostly undertaken by government agencies, but landlords with a large labour force at their disposal also frequently undertook the embanking and draining of such new lands. . . . The large scale of operations of the owners of *chuang-yüan* and their great reserves of wealth also enabled them to capitalize their operations on a scale far beyond the reach of the small individual farmer. The Sung, and in particular the twelfth and thirteenth centuries, was a period of rapid improvement in agricultural techniques and of the invention of new implements. The great landlords of the lower Yangtse valley installed complex water-driven machinery for pumping irrigation water, for draining their fields, and for threshing and milling their grain. They also invested in the large variety of improved and complicated field implements which are described and illustrated in the rich literature on agricultural techniques published during the late Sung and Yüan.

The officials themselves also began actively to encourage increased rural productivity, and in the place of the conventional Confucian homilies extolling the virtues of hard labour which they were accustomed to address to the people of their district, we find them instructing the farmers in the use of new techniques. Through the government agencies new early ripening varieties both of wheat and of rice were widely disseminated. The use of a wide range of manures, including lime, vast quantities of human waste from the ever-growing cities, and manure crops grown to be ploughed in, became universal.

The tenant farmers themselves played an important role in increasing productivity. Since their contracts normally defined the rent as a fixed proportion of their rice crop they commonly began to grow a double grain crop of autumn-sown wheat of an early-ripening variety followed by spring-sown rice. The wheat was grown purely as a cash-crop for sale in the cities of the lower Yangtse area, where a huge market in grain swiftly grew up. The cities also provided an insatiable market for every variety of vegetable and other food products raised specially for sale.

The *chuang-yüan* were in fact an essential feature in the boom of agrarian productivity which, it is becoming increasingly evident, characterized the late Sung, at least in southern and central China. Without this great increase in productivity, it is difficult to imagine how the splendours of the capital at Hang-chou and of the other great cities, which so impressed Marco Polo, could have arisen, or how the state could have continued to provide the enormous sums which it spent upon defence during the wars with the Chin and later with the Mongols, even after the loss to the Chinese of all northern China during the twelfth century.

4

THE CITY IN TRADITIONAL CHINESE CIVILIZATION

Frederick W. Mote

L. Hilbersheimer has described how medieval European cities developed from villages, and what basic urban functions typically came to be embodied in their form:

> Cities were much like villages at first, but they soon began to show the characteristics of urban development, industrial, political and architectural. Cities had to protect themselves with fortifications. They had to have a city hall, a place of assembly where citizens could exercise their political rights. There had to be a church also, eventually perhaps a cathedral, a place of worship dominating the city both spiritually and architecturally.[1]

Very little in this description holds true for the traditional Chinese city. It is striking that in the case of the medieval and pre-modern European city, the organizational and psychological separateness from its countryside was clearly attested to in physical monuments, and those dominated the city. The Chinese city, in contrast, had no "citizens," nor any corporate identity, and the authority under which it was directly administrated extended beyond the city to

 This selection was written for this volume and is based upon the author's essay "The Transformation of Nanking, 1350–1400," to be published in *The City in Imperial China*, edited by G. William Skinner (Stanford University Press).

[1] *The Nature of Cities* (Chicago: Paul Theobald and Company, 1955), p. 90.

include the surrounding countryside. It had therefore no need of a town hall as a monument to urban pride and urban group identity, or as a place of assembly where citizens could exercise political rights. Not even the defense of the Chinese city was a responsibility of the urban entity; its defenses were constituted and maintained by the central government to which all alike were subservient, and as part of its nation-wide defense installation.

Nor were there comparable physical monuments of the religious element of Chinese life. On the one hand, China lacked the concept of sacred cities or holy public shrines. Its state cult was the private business of the Chinese Emperor; its important physical monuments were his ancestral temple and altars of the state in his palace precincts, the altars of heaven and earth in the suburbs of the capital where only he could function as priest, and the tombs of his and previous dynasties' imperial ancestors, which were invariably in rural, often quite remote settings. On the other hand, although public religion had many and pervasive manifestations, it was simply not comparable in terms of organization, or financing, or in any links with the city as the place where its monuments attested to its role in society. Both Buddhist and Taoist churches had nominal national hierarchies; in fact, however, both religions existed in atomized structure, and each temple was an independent unit. There were no religious authorities comparable to bishops or archbishops, no diocesan or synodal structures of authority, no institutional bases to function like cathedrals or chapterhouses. It is true that every city and town had its important temples. Those we call the Confucian Temples or Temples of Literature were in fact state offices; they were important chiefly for their secular functions. Buddhist and Taoist temples had to be licensed by the state, which was normally rather unsympathetic towards them, at times suppressive. They could be closed or required to move by secular authority. Although temples located in cities frequently were rich and splendid, and their pagodas or great halls very often were the tallest structures on the low and spreading profile of the Chinese city, we can scarcely say that they dominated it spiritually or architecturally. Temples in rural settings, in any event, were often still larger, richer, more ornate. The great European church buildings are identified with city life, with relatively few exceptions. The great and enduring centers of Chinese religions on the other hand are not marked by permanent architectural monuments of stone and glass, and characteristically (although not exclusively) they have been in remote rural, often mountain settings.

Most important of all in this comparison is the fact that the cities of China were not keystones in an important religious institutional structure, a state within the state as in Europe, or an arm of the state as in ancient Egypt and the classical and the Islamic worlds. That deprived the Chinese city of one of the elements that contributed most conspicuously to the importance of cities elsewhere.

Religion's organizational forms and physical monuments provide one striking point of contrast between the Chinese city and the pre-modern city in the West. Other characteristics of the Chinese city suggest still further links between its physical components and the distinctive organizational basis of Chinese life. The architectural peculiarities of the Chinese city offer suggestive clues. Chinese urban houses, business buildings, temples, and government structures, even in the concentrations of highest density, remained essentially one-story structures or combinations of one- and two-story parts forming single units. The profile of the Chinese city was therefore flat. Moreover, the parts of a single unit, be it small house or large official building, were arranged to enclose and to include the use of open space. Exposure to air and sun was essential to the design of buildings. In such essentials of design, in materials used, in style and ornamentation, Chinese urban structures were indistinguishable from rural structures. Traditional Chinese architecture included no such things as "town house" style, or "country church" style, or "city office" style. They were not needed. Nor did the Chinese city force structures up into the air in the manner of the four- and six-story burghers' houses in old European cities, or the tenements of ancient Rome. The pressure on space, even in later imperial times, failed to remove from the city its courtyards and gardens as it tended to do in Renaissance and modern Europe. The Chinese city did not totally lack, but had less need of, public squares and public gardens; its citizens, in striking contrast, had and probably preferred to use their small, private, but open and sunny courtyards.

The continuum from city to suburbs to open countryside thus

was manifested in the uniformity of building styles and of layout and use of ground space. Neither the city wall nor the actual limits of the suburban concentration marked the city off from the countryside in architectural terms. Nor did styles of dress, patterns of food and drink, means of transportation, or any other obvious aspect of daily life display characteristic dichotomies of urban and rural.

Lewis Mumford, in *The Culture of Cities* (1938), has observed that cities in the West have served as museums of man's past, as molds of the successive stages of his civilization, holding up for view, in their physical monuments, the record of outgrown styles and superseded modes of life. "In the city," he has remarked, "time becomes visible: buildings and monuments and public ways more open than the written record, more subject to the gaze of many men than the scattered artifacts of the countryside, leave an imprint on the minds even of the ignorant or the indifferent. Through the material fact of preservation, time challenges time, time clashes with time; habits and values carry over beyond the living group, streaking with different strata of time the character of any single generation." He regards the variety in urban period styles as an important source of stimulus to change in civilization. He states: "By the diversity of its time-structures, the city in part escapes the tyranny of a single present, or the monotony of a future that consists in repeating only a single beat heard in the past. . . ." (page 4).

Much of what Mumford so effectively observed about the creativity of cities, and about their significance for cultural continuity, is true of Chinese cities and no doubt of all cities; that is, the concentration of physical monuments in the urban setting left its profound imprint on the consciousness of the reviewer. That helped to make him aware of his society and of his cultural traditions. Yet again, in a striking way the Chinese city is an exception to the most important point he has raised: the Chinese city did not possess visible "diversity of its time-structures." Time did not challenge time as Chinese man viewed his urban streets. If in China there was no danger that the past would not preserve itself, neither did the architectural monuments remind the viewer of specific time-styles in the past. Architecturally, the present was never strikingly new or different. No Chinese building was obviously dateable in terms of period styles. No Chinese city ever had the equivalent of a Romanesque or a Gothic past to be overlaid by a burst of Classical renascence; none today has a Victorian nightmare to be scorned in an age of functionalism, except in so far as Victorian imports still exist in some of the concession areas of the old treaty-ports. In that sense, the Chinese city did not "escape the tyranny of a single present," but neither did it consider "a future that consists in repeating only a single beat heard in the past" to be monotonous. Nor, in fact, was it monotonous to the Chinese viewer, intent upon other nuances. What this suggests about the continuum in time may be extended to the rural-urban continuum in space, and to the problem of defining the boundaries of the Chinese city.

It would be a mistake to exaggerate the Chinese urban-rural uniformities, to be sure. Yet, the cultural life of the civilization, in particular in later imperial China from Sung times onward, appears not to have fallen into two widely divergent spheres that we can label the urban and the rural. In part this reflects the rural ideals of the upper classes, the permeation of these ideals throughout the whole society, and the tendency of the upper classes to live ambivalently in both town and country. It is easy to focus on and therefore to over-interpret the life of the educated upper classes; it is very difficult to extend our knowledge to the masses of the people. Nonetheless it is significant to observe that the lives and the cultural activities of the elite were not in any sense confined to the cities. Within the lower levels of society there probably were much more clearly identifiable "urbanites" and "ruralites," and no doubt the distinction between city and country must have had much more meaning in the pattern of their daily lives. Even so, Chinese cities were not beleaguered islands in a sea of barbarism, and the spatial continuity of cultural tone certainly reflects aspects of the organization of society.

Because of their concentration of people and of wealth, and their greater possibilities for division of labor and specialization, traditional Chinese cities could of course support some cultural activities that were not possible in the countryside. Some of the arts and crafts and proto-sciences depended on shops and markets, goods and craftsmen, and the patronage of densely concentrated populations. This point is obvious, and fits our expectations about the roles of cities in cultural history. Yet again, however, it is the qualifications on this obvious fact that are important; we must hesitate before making the too-easy analogies with other times and places. For example, Chinese schools were in cities in the case of government institutions (the exceptions being some famous private academies in rural settings that became recipients of government subsidies and thereafter functioned as semiofficial schools). But characteristically the private academies which in later imperial history often functioned as chief centers of intellectual activity, were more often than not located in villages or out-of-the-way rural settings until perhaps the eighteenth and nineteenth centuries. Publishing activities frequently were not in the major cities; some of the most important of them were located at the village properties of their scholar-official owners. Government offices and government schools usually had small libraries, and these to be sure were located in walled cities. But the great libraries (except for those belonging to the imperial court) were private, and they often were located in the rural village or small town properties of their gentry owners. Private art collections also frequently were housed in the rural villas of the rich. Scholars, poets, thinkers, writers, and artists customarily were in public life for portions of their lives, and hence in these years were necessarily residents of cities, and away from their native places. But their productive years often were the years of their private life when, in China, they not only were not concentrated in one or two great cities of the realm, but were widely dispersed and very apt to be residing in rural places.

These features of Chinese cultural life probably did not exist in any equivalent fashion in the cultural life of Europe or the Classical world. Perhaps we can formulate the concept of a culturally "open" situation in China. That is, Chinese cultural activities involved both the cities and the countryside, they were indistinguishably "urban" or "rural," and they reflected attitudes toward city and country that were different from those in pre-modern Europe, where a few great cities tended to monopolize a more "confined" cultural life.

Similarly, it appears that the concept of the "provincial" as opposed to the "metropolitan" did not exist in China as it did in the cultural life of Europe. Careers in the national capitals were, to be sure, different in character and prestige from those in the provinces. But in the cultural life of the nation, there was not the same gulf between the capital city and the provinces. Some of the Chinese provinces were culturally inferior, especially those more distant or more recently sinofied, such as Kweichow and Yunnan. But the cultural life of some of the Yangtze Valley provinces was recognized as being superior to that of the capital and the provinces adjacent to it. In the Yuan period the cultural life of China continued to center in the lower Yangtze area even though the political capital was Ta-tu, modern Peking. And thereafter, through the Ming and Ch'ing periods, even though the dynastic capital created at Nanking in 1368 was moved to Peking after 1420, the provinces of the Yangtze area obviously rivaled or surpassed the northern capital as centers of culture; they in fact exceeded it in overall richness of cultural life. Thus not all the provinces were "provincial" in a cultural sense. This reinforces the point about the dispersion of Chinese cultural life throughout the empire and throughout both city and countryside.

Were we to examine the organization of economic life, we would find that in some ways it paralleled the dispersion of cultural activities. For example, many of the most flourishing market areas and commercial concentrations were outside of city walls, if adjacent to major cities. Some beginnings of "national markets," such as the Wu-hu rice market, were located not in major cities but in small-town locations. Some of the principal beginnings of industrialism were centered in market towns rather than in major cities (e.g., ceramics at Ching-te-chen and iron works at Fatshan), while others were dispersed throughout a region, creating proto-proletariats of small-town or even rural residence (e.g., the cotton textile industry in southeastern Kiangsu) even when the industry's organizational nexus may have been urban-based. Moreover, China's major economic centers as such appear to have been widely dispersed, and not centered in the three or four principal cities of the realm.

Our case for an urban-rural continuum in traditional China thus rests upon evidence from the physical form of cities, from styles in architecture and dress, from evidence about urban and rural attitudes in elite (and perhaps in popular) psychology, from the structure and character of cultural activities, and even from some glimpses into the pattern of economic life. It suggests that cities, important concentrations of Chinese life, related to the whole of China's national existence in ways that differ from our expectations about the pre-modern city elsewhere.

5

THE ISSUE OF CAPITALISM IN CHINA

Etienne Balazs

There is, or should be, a consensus of opinion today about the structure of Chinese society before the Western impact, or at least about its main features. A huge agrarian country, the vast majority of its inhabitants were peasants. There was a comparatively small middle class of handicraftsmen and merchants. And finally, at the top of the structure was a thin layer of scholar-officials, the ruling class. These famous literati, often called gentry, small in number but of immense power, dominated Chinese society for more than 2,000 years. I don't like and don't recommend the term "gentry," because in this society more landed property was acquired through office than office was acquired through ownership of landed property. Of course, being a landowner gave one a better chance of obtaining the education necessary for office. But the position of the landed aristocracy was shaken by the introduction of a civil service and of the literary examination system from the eighth century A.D. onward.

* * *

The relations between the officials and the merchant class were stamped by the fact that the officials, in their capacity as the ruling class—endowed with learning that enabled them to supervise and coordinate the activities of an agrarian society, and thus to acquire their dominant position in the state—enjoyed an all-pervading power and prestige. In these relations, as seen from above, every means of keeping the merchant class down and holding it in subjection seemed permissible. Compromises, exceptions, favors, pardons—all were allowed so long as they were retracted at the earliest opportunity. Claims, titles, privileges, immunities, deeds, charters were never granted. Any sign of initiative in the other camp was usually strangled at birth, or if it had reached a stage when it could no longer be suppressed, the state laid hands on it, took it under control, and appropriated the resultant profits. As seen from below, there was, in these relations, no legal way of obtaining an immunity, a franchise, since the state and its representatives, the officials, were almighty. There remained only an indirect way of obtaining one's due: bribery.

The outstanding feature in these relations is the absence of pluck, the complete lack of a fighting spirit, on the part of the middle class. On the one hand, they felt impotent in the face of a competitor who seemed to hold all the advantages. On the other, they had no real desire to be different, to oppose their own way of life to that of the ruling class—and this inhibited them even more. Their ambition was limited: to find a position, if only a modest one, inside the ruling class, reflecting the social prestige attached to officialdom. Their consuming desire was that they, or their children, should become scholar-officials. . . .

Let me illustrate what has so far been said with a few examples chosen at random.

Private initiative was responsible for the invention of the first instruments of credit. In the eighth century A.D., under the T'ang dynasty, when commercial activities were expanding rapidly, merchants found that large-scale transfer of cash was cumbersome, laborious, and perilous. They invented "flying money," by means of which merchants, on depositing cash at certain specified offices, received a written receipt guaranteeing reimbursement in other provinces. In 811 the government prohibited the use of flying money by private citizens and adopted the system for its own credit transfers. Merchants were allowed to deposit cash at government finance offices in the capital against payments to be received in the provinces. A 10 per cent fee was charged on the drafts.

During roughly the same period, the Buddhists invented printing for the purpose of religious propaganda. The state took over this invention and used it for the contrary purpose of diffusing the Confucian doctrine, and then proceeded to persecute the Buddhist church—not, it is true, because of this, but for several other reasons.

The first protobanks to issue promissory notes, which soon became a kind of paper currency, were founded by rich merchants in Szechwan, which was one of the trading centers during the eleventh century. To begin with, the government recognized sixteen of the larger merchants, and granted them a monopoly in the issue of these "exchange media" (*chiao-tzu*), which brought in a fee of 3 per cent. But a few years later, in A.D. 1023, a government monopoly replaced the private monopoly. . . .

In the Sung period merchants' guilds were obliged to supply government needs on demand. This obligation was the cause for many grievances, because the price paid by the government was lower than the market price, and the merchant whose turn it was to supply the goods had himself to pay the transport costs. At the petition of the butchers' guild in the capital, the government granted, in A.D. 1073, a kind of "privilege," according to which members of the corporations were to pay a monthly fee for exemption from this obligation and the government was to pay the market price for the goods. Twelve years later, however, the state returned to the former system. One of the reasons for this setback is quite typical. The guilds forced petty merchants to join the corporation if they had not yet done so in order that they would share the burden of paying the exemption fee. . . .

It is not fortuitous that these examples I have chosen should all come from late T'ang or Sung times, for this was the period during which urban development went hand in hand with intense commercial activity. We are therefore compelled to look for the germs of capitalism as early as the latter half of the eighth century. But in doing so, we must never forget the essential difference between

Chinese and Western towns—of which my last example is a case in point. The difference is this: while the Western town was the seedbed and later the bulwark of the bourgeoisie, the Chinese town was primarily the seat of government, the residence of officials who were permanently hostile to the bourgeoisie, and thus always under the domination of the state.

Nor is it a matter of chance that the first great thrust of the Chinese bourgeoisie happened during a period—late T'ang and more especially Sung times—when national sovereignty was divided. It is my firm belief that whenever national sovereignty was divided, and the power of the state and the ruling scholar-officials was consequently weakened, the middle class flourished as a result. Other instances apart from the Sung period are provided by the lively, brilliant epoch of the Warring States in ancient times and, during the Middle Ages, the period of the Three Kingdoms and of the division of China between the northern barbarian and the southern national dynasties. But even in times which favored the merchants, the state and the state monopolies were a heavy drag on commercial activities.

This can be illustrated in greater detail by mining and the salt industry, which afford typical examples of how the workings of early capitalism in China were hampered by bureaucratic regulations. Both were outstandingly thriving enterprises, in which the largest fortunes were acquired. Yet both, together with the tea trade, foreign trade, and military supplies, were more or less equally prosperous whether they operated under state license, state control, or state monopoly. . . .

The salt monopoly had always been a major source of revenue for the Chinese state. Taxes on consumer goods are attested as early as the sixth century B.C. From T'ang times on, the *gabelle* produced a large proportion of the state revenue. In order to enforce the monopoly against smugglers and make the salt industry a going concern, the government had recourse to merchants to distribute salt, as this was too cumbersome an undertaking for the state agencies to carry out, particularly with a growing increase in population.

Under the last dynasty, the salt tax amounted yearly to about five million taels. Originally half the amount of the salt tax—and after the middle of the eighteenth century 40 per cent of it—was collected in the largest and richest of the eleven salt administration areas of middle and southeast China, called Liang-Huai. Thanks to the existence of a large number of documents, it is possible to calculate that the Liang-Huai traders—those "unchallenged merchant princes of China"—distributed annually to 75 million people (a quarter of the total population in the eighteenth century) more than 600 million pounds of salt, with an average annual profit of about seven million taels. Let us see how this trade worked and what became of the money earned by the merchants.

The salt masters were originally small independent manufacturers who had a small but quick return and no risk; but during the eighteenth century they came more and more under the sway of the wholesale dealers. By 1800, only half of them remained owners of salterns, and even when they were the legal owners of their small manufacturing works, they were in fact wage earners under the control of the capitalists. The wholesale dealers at first only bought salt from the owner-manufacturers and sold it to the salt distributors, but later they became large-scale producers. As such, they ran a considerable risk because of the perishable nature of salt. Salt was stored for a year before being sold to the transport merchants. The factory merchants bought up the property of bankrupt salt masters, or shared profits with them as joint owners. These factory merchants owed their position to government recognition. Only thirty of them were recognized, and . . . they were able to keep tight control not only over the manufacturers, but also over the small-scale merchants, who were often their agents. The producers made an annual profit of about one-and-a-half to two million taels, of which they pocketed 60 per cent, leaving the remaining 40 per cent to be divided half-and-half between the depot merchants and the salt makers.

Profits were even higher on the distribution side of the trade. The transport merchants made about five million taels annually. . . . The established practice, typical of the whole organization, which remained in operation until the middle of the nineteenth century, was as follows. The inalienable right to sell salt was farmed out to rich merchants who could pay the gabelle in advance; the names of these licensed monopoly merchants were entered in an official register, called the shipment register (*kang-ts'e*), because the annual quota of salt distributed in the Liang-Huai area was divided into so many shipments.

The organization of these transport merchants, of whom there were only 230 in Liang-Huai, is a revelation for anyone interested in Chinese capitalism. There were, in fact, only thirty head merchants, half of them owners of the monopoly license, the other half only leaseholders. They were responsible for arrears in tax payment and for the conduct of the whole merchant body, that is, for the 200 retailers—"small" men compared with the head merchants, but mostly men of substantial means, usually required to trade under the name of one of the head merchants. They were milked by the head merchants by two main devices: the high rate of interest on loaned capital, and the practice of shifting the burden of "squeeze" to the entire group of transport merchants; meanwhile, the head merchants appropriated a large share of the "treasury fee" (*hsia*). The treasury fee was money for expenses incurred in entertaining officials and for contributions to local administration; it was paid out of the common treasury of the entire merchant body, but handled exclusively by a few merchant treasurers. This practice was of course encouraged by high officials in the salt administration, who shared the fat bonus with these few merchants. . . . The heirarchy, with all its tensions of give and take, stands out clearly enough: high officials → local administration → merchant chiefs → head merchants → small merchants. And below them, of course, were the consumers—the peasants who bore the burden of the tax.

We come now at long last to the crucial question of accumulation. What did the salt merchants do with the enormous profits gained during the years of high prosperity, profits estimated at 250 million taels for the second half of the eighteenth century? Let us first answer another question: where did the merchants come from and how did they live? . . . For those who recall the connection established by Max Weber between the austere Puritan tradition of thrift and early capitalism, the following passage from a description of China about A.D. 1600 will have a familiar ring:

> The rich men of the empire in the regions south of the Yangtze are from Hsin-an [ancient name of Hui-chou], in the regions north of that river, from Shansi. The great merchants of Hui-chou have made fisheries and salt their occupation and have amassed fortunes amounting to one million taels of silver. Others with a fortune of two or three hundred thousand can only rank as middle merchants. The Shansi merchants are engaged in salt, silk, reselling of grain. Their wealth even exceeds that of the former. This is because the Hui-chou merchants are extravagant, but those of *Shansi are frugal.* In fact, *people of Hui-chou are also extremely miserly as to food and clothing,* . . . but with regard to concubines, prostitutes and lawsuits, they squander gold like dust.

The descendants of these hard-working and frugal men, in the second or third generation after the original fortune had been made, acquired very different habits. They became status seekers, spending fabulous sums in an endless quest for social prestige. Their response to the ruling-class principle of "keeping tradesmen in their place" was to compensate for lack of social prestige by ostentatious living. They indulged in eccentricities and expensive hobbies, "dogs, horses, music, and women"; they owned beautiful pleasure gardens; they became bibliophiles, collectors, and art connoisseurs; they patronized and subsidized scholars on a lavish scale and held veritable literary salons. Dozens of famous literati . . . were their guests and protégés. And it is certainly a fact that, even allowing for the not entirely voluntary contribution of 41 million taels to the imperial treasury (for the emperor's personal expenses) during the second half of the eighteenth century, their mode of life, clan solidarity, and expenses for education diverted most of the accumulated capital to noneconomic uses.

Another impediment to the development of capitalism was the traditionally preferred investment in land. Although the rent from land probably amounted to no more than 30 to 40 per cent of the return from businesses such as pawnbroking, moneylending, and shopkeeping, we find that the laws of the Peking club of the townsmen from Hui-chou—the famous Hsin-an merchants—decreed that any unused public funds of the club "should be invested in the purchase of real estate for receipt of rent, and should not be lent for interest, *in order to avoid risks.*" "Small risk and high prestige were two major factors which had made investment in land attractive." . . .

The following points may serve as a summary of the arguments presented above.

First: I can give no exact date for the birth of capitalism in China. All I know is that the tendency will be to set this date further and further back, from the nineteenth to the eighteenth to the seventeenth century and so on, finally arriving at the Sung dynasty (tenth to thirteenth centuries), which in my opinion marks the beginning of modern times in China. Still, the discontinuity just mentioned distorts the steady, simple, ascending line so much favored by school textbooks.

Second: with regard to industrial capitalism, we must never forget that the purpose of machines is to economize labor or time. In China there was never any dearth of labor; on the contrary, China always had plenty of it. The superabundance of cheap labor certainly hampered the search for time-saving devices. Nevertheless, what was chiefly lacking in China for the further development of capitalism was not mechanical skill or scientific aptitude, nor a sufficient accumulation of wealth, but scope for individual enterprise. There was no individual freedom and no security for private enterprise, no legal foundation for rights other than those of the state, no alternative investment other than landed property, no guarantee against being penalized by arbitrary exactions from officials or against intervention by the state. But perhaps the supreme inhibiting factor was the overwhelming prestige of the state bureaucracy, which maimed from the start any attempt of the bourgeoisie to be different, to become aware of themselves as a class and fight for an autonomous position in society. Free enterprise, ready and proud to take risks, is therefore quite exceptional and abnormal in Chinese economic history.

Third: if capitalism is interpreted as meaning only competitive capitalism, or free enterprise (which has nearly disappeared in our world), then there never has been capitalism in China. But if state capitalism is admitted as forming an integral and important part of the phenomenon we call capitalism, then it appears to us in China as a hoary old man who has left to his sturdy and reckless great grandson a stock of highly valuable experiences.

And just because we live in the epoch of state capitalism, both in the old capitalist countries of the West and in the new "People's Democracies" of the East, the matter is one of great relevance to us today.

6

SOCIAL MOBILITY IN CHINA SINCE THE FOURTEENTH CENTURY

Ping-ti Ho

Social stratification in traditional China was based in general on the Mencian principle that those who labor with their mind rule and those who labor with their physical strength are ruled. But this was only a broad principle which did not coincide exactly with the actual stratificational practice. We have found that throughout the past two thousand years not all those who labored with their mind were members of the ruling class, nor was traditional Chinese society a two-class society. While it is partially true that social stratification in Ming-Ch'ing society differs somewhat from that in the modern West because high statuses were determined primarily by higher academic degrees and position in the bureaucracy, yet the power of money was increasingly felt. Before 1450 money could indirectly help its possessor to attain higher academic degrees and statuses; after 1451 money could be directly translated into higher statuses through the purchase of studentships, offices, and official titles. This is partially shown by statistics on the initial qualifications of Ch'ing officials . . . and the high ratios of academic success of salt-merchant families. . . . In the light of our knowledge of late Ch'ing institutional history it may indeed be said that money, after 1850 at the latest, had overshadowed higher academic degrees as a determinant of higher statuses. Since education has become increas-

From *The Ladder of Success in Imperial China: Aspects of Social Mobility, 1368–1911* by Ping-ti Ho (New York: Columbia University Press, 1960), pp. 40–43, 51–52, 256–62. Excerpted by permission of the publisher. The original footnotes have been deleted.

ingly important as a determinant of social status in the advanced industrial societies of the modern West, we find that between late Ch'ing times and the rise of Communism in China in 1949 social stratification in China and in the West became increasingly similar.

Although the Ming-Ch'ing society, like the Chinese society of earlier periods, was a regulated society, we have found that the discrepancy between the social ideals embodied in legal texts and social realities was a very great one. Legally, the early Ming state prescribed that certain special-service statuses be hereditary; in fact, the complex social and economic forces, together with the lack of strong will on the part of the imperial government strictly to enforce the stringent law, made the maintenance of such special statuses impossible. In the Ming-Ch'ing period as a whole, the status system was fluid and flexible and there were no effective legal and social barriers which prevented the movement of individuals and families from one status to another.

The fluidity of the status system is partially shown by Ming statistics . . . but mainly by various types of nonquantifiable evidence ranging from biographies and genealogies to social novels and the comments of contemporary observers on clan and family affairs. So common was the fact that trade and other productive occupations either alternated or were synchronized with studies that many Ming-Ch'ing social observers were of the impression that the status distinction among the four major occupational categories (scholars, peasants, artisans, and merchants) was blurred. What is more, all types of literature agree that the most striking characteristic of the post-T'ang society was that, on one hand, social success depended more on individual merit than on family status, and that, on the other hand, high-status families had little means of perpetuating their success if their descendants were inept. Hence the long series of social observers from Sung times onward who formulated the theory of human environment as the most important factor in social success and propagated the typically post-T'ang pessimistic social view that wealth and glory were inconstant. In the light of the evidence presented in chapters IV and V, these impressions and views are by and large justified. For during the Ming-Ch'ing period there were various institutionalized and noninstitutional channels which promoted the upward mobility of the humble and obscure but there were few institutionalized means to prevent the long-range downward mobility of successful families. In this sense, the Ming-Ch'ing society was highly competitive in its peculiar ways. . . .

Wang Ting-pao, a late T'ang *chin-shih*[1] and the author of interesting anecdotes on the T'ang examination system, told the story that the great T'ang emperor T'ai-tsung (reigned 627–49), after seeing the theatrical and august procession of the newly graduated *chin-shih,* remarked with gratification: "The world's men of unusual ambitions have thus been trapped in my bag!" Whether T'ang T'ai-tsung, from whose reign onward the examination system was regularly held, had indeed made this remark cannot easily be proved, because Wang lived nearly three centuries later. But this anecdote is indicative of what late T'ang Chinese, after having observed the political and social effect of the examination for more than two centuries, believed to have been the real purpose of the early T'ang state in making it a permanent system. In any case, subsequent rulers, especially the Ming founder, well understood that a certain degree of constant social circulation was vital to the stability of the dynasty. In fact, the examination system's long history of thirteen centuries is a most eloquent testimonial to its usefulness as a main channel of mobility and as a politically and socially stabilizing factor. . . .

Although this study deals with the last two dynasties in Chinese history, it may be useful in the final consideration to make some observations on the important changes in Chinese society and social mobility over a longer period. In retrospect, the T'ang period was an important transition during which the monopoly of political power by the early-medieval hereditary aristocracy was gradually broken up under the impact of the competitive examination system. The fact that there was more social circulation during the T'ang than during the previous three centuries cannot be much doubted, although it is difficult to say whether the truly humble and poor had much chance of social success. Very little is known of the precise family background of prominent T'ang Chinese who owed their success to the examination. Even when T'ang literature and

[1] [Those who were given third (National) degree in the civil-service examination.]

biographies refer to an individual's social origin as humble or lowly, the adjective must be interpreted in the T'ang social context. It is probable that such adjectives as humble and lowly were used by contemporaries only in comparison with the hereditary aristocratic clans which, if they were no longer able to monopolize political power from the mid-seventh century onward, remained the dominant political factor and enjoyed unrivaled social prestige down to the very end of the T'ang period.

After the great T'ang clans finally declined amidst the incessant wars of the Five Dynasties (907–60) and the perpetuation of the examination system under the Sung (960–1279), Chinese society definitely became more mobile and the social composition of the ruling bureaucracy more broadened. . . .

The trend of increasing mobility continued after the founding of the Ming, when the examination and academic degree system became more elaborate and the school system truly nationwide. All this, together with the most unusual political and social circumstances in which the Ming dynasty was inaugurated, created a chapter of social mobility probably unparalleled in Chinese history. One of the important findings of this study is that Category A *chin-shih* figures were highest at the beginning of Ming times gradually became stabilized at a high level during the fifteenth and the greater part of the sixteenth centuries, began to decline drastically in the late sixteenth century, and further dropped to a stabilized low level of below 20 percent after the late seventeenth century. Other things being equal, members of successful families naturally had various competitive advantages and must in the long run prevail over the humble and poor in the competitive examination. It would appear that the chances of successful mobility for ordinary commoners would have begun to decline drastically earlier had it not been for the combined effect of the early stage of large-scale reproduction of basic classics and reference tools, the teachings of Wang Yang-ming, and the subsequent mushrooming growth of private academies. The rise of a large number of private academies, with their usual scholarship provisions, occurred just about the time that community schools had begun to decline.

The early Manchu rulers, unlike the Ming founder who came

from a poor peasant family, were mainly concerned with winning the support of the key social class in their conquered land, namely, the scholar-official class. With the exception of the Shun-chih period (1644–61), when the unusually large *chin-shih* quotas helped to maintain the Category A figures at the late Ming level, the chances of social success for ordinary commoners were continually being reduced because of the restrictive *chin-shih* quotas and the rapid multiplication of the national population, with its eventual grave economic consequences. Although the average Ch'ing Category A recruitment ratio was still not insubstantial, the consequence of this much curtailed opportunity-structure for the humble and obscure must be assessed in the Chinese social context of the time. For a nation which in the light of Ming experience had come to believe in a sort of academic Horatio Alger myth, the facts and factors reflected in the persistent downward trend in Category A series must have engendered a widespread sense of social frustration. It seems pertinent to speculate whether this has had anything to do with the increasing social unrest and revolutions that have characterized nineteenth- and twentieth-century China. It was perhaps more than coincidental that the Taiping rebellion, the most massive civil war in world history, was precipitated by Hung Hsiu-ch'üan (1813–64), a member of a small landowning peasant family who had repeatedly failed to obtain his first degree. It ought to be pointed out, however, that while during the greater part of the Ch'ing period the rulers' "bag" had obviously failed to trap sufficient numbers of the socially ambitious, the rebellion engineered by one of the frustrated made possible a brief chapter of increased social mobility. . . .

Since in the field of Chinese studies the term "gentry" has become very popular in recent years, a brief discussion of the term itself is necessary. As is well known, gentry is a typically English term which from Tudor times onward acquired rather concrete social, economic, and political connotations. In the sixteenth, seventeenth, and eighteenth centuries members of the English gentry owned large landed estates, controlled or dominated county administration, and, from the late eighteenth century onward, were mostly Tory in their political sympathies. Some keen contemporary French observers of

English society could find no French or continental European analogy to these English gentry, whom they called "nobiles minores," an appellation with an aristocratic aroma. Within certain limits it is of course permissible to borrow a foreign term, but when the realities behind the borrowed term are so remote from the social, economic, and political contexts of the original, there is strong reason to reject the term altogether. Since the most important determinant of English gentry status was landed property and sometimes other forms of wealth, there is danger in borrowing it as a generic term for the Chinese class of officials and potential officials who, during a greater part of the Ming-Ch'ing period, owed their status only partly to wealth but mostly to an academic degree. Furthermore, it is difficult to equate broadly the Chinese class of officials and potential officials with the English gentry because many of the officials and potential officials of the lower bureaucratic stratum were actually men of relatively modest circumstances and a far cry from "nobiles minores." They should be regarded as a key class only in the peculiar context of the Ming-Ch'ing society.

To sum up the composition of the official class in its broad sense, in Ming times it includes officials, active, retired, expectant, and potential; subofficials, *chin-shih, chü-jen, kung-sheng,* both regular and irregular; and *chien-sheng*. The Ch'ing period official class is the same except for the *chien-sheng,* which is excluded. *Sheng-yüan*[2] are regarded for the whole Ming-Ch'ing period as a significant socially transitional group among commoners. While no demarcation between the broadly defined official class and commoners can be completely free from arbitrariness, the many-sided evidence presented above, and much else that would be repetitious, shows that our demarcation is in the main justified in terms of both legal and social stratifications. . . .

[2] *Sheng-yüan*—those who were given the first (local) degree in the civil service examination.

Chien-sheng—those who were given the first degree in the civil service examination and conferred with high honor.

Kung-sheng—those who were given the first degree in the civil service examination and conferred with highest honor.

Chü-jen—those who were given the second (provincial) degree in the civil service examination.

This leads us to another fundamental problem of social stratification in Ming-Ch'ing China, namely, the relative importance of education (or its more concrete expression: opportunities for government service) and wealth as determinants of social status. Since government statutes and documents deal mainly with legal stratification, subtler social realities must be sought in social novels and private literary writings. Granted that some of the cases given below are perhaps too extreme to be accepted as a reflection of the general social truth, such extreme cases will nevertheless help to sharpen our theoretical perception of the relative importance of an office or a potential office and of wealth as determinants of social status. We will arrive at a more balanced view after these extreme cases are interpreted against some statistics which reflect the general social pattern.

We are fortunate in having a most revealing and realistic social novel *An Unofficial History of the Literati,* a work which is indispensable for the study of that key social class in Ming-Ch'ing society. One of the many illuminating episodes concerns an indigent southern scholar, Fan Chin, who for years lived partially at the mercy of his father-in-law, a bullying and cursing butcher. When the news that he had passed the provincial examination arrived, he was so stunned and choked with emotion that he temporarily lost his senses. Since the butcher had previously inflicted physical pain on Fan to bring him back to his senses, some neighbors suggested that he should do it again. But the butcher no longer dared because he believed that his son-in-law, now a *chü-jen,* must have been the reincarnation of one of the stars in heaven. This second degree, which entitled Fan to an eventual office, was charismatic in more than one way; it completely transformed his economic and social status overnight. A local retired county magistrate, himself a holder of the *chü-jen* degree, immediately called and offered Fan a large house and some ready cash. Soon the smaller men of the locality offered Fan either a part of their land, shares of their stores, or themselves as domestic servants—all in the hope of gaining his favor and protection.

An episode in another social novel, *The Marriage that Awakens the World,* differs only in minor detail. It is about the sudden change of fortune of Ch'ao Ssu-hsiao, for years a *sheng-yüan* and man of limited property. After having failed repeatedly to attain the *chü-jen* degree he eventually became a *kung-sheng* through seniority. This graduate status enabled him to take a special examination for minor government office. He passed it and was to be appointed a county magistrate. This news was sufficient to induce some of the local poor to offer themselves as his domestic servants, certain local "middle-class" people to transfer to him the title deeds of their property, and money-lender's to make loans to him with nominal or no interest. The Ch'ao family suddenly became one of the richest and most powerful in the district. These two episodes, given independently by a southern and a northern novelist, indicate that a higher degree often led to sudden elevation in both economic and social status. . . .

By way of summing up, it is clear from our illustrations and from general statistics that money in Ming-Ch'ing China was not in itself an ultimate source of power. It had to be translated into official status to make its power fully felt. From the founding of the Ming to the Mongol invasion of 1449 wealth could indirectly help in the attainment of a higher degree and an official appointment. The sporadic sales of offices after 1451 opened up a new channel of social mobility for the well-to-do and made money an increasingly important factor in the determination of social status. But up to the outbreak of the Taiping rebellion in 1851 the state had always made the examination system the primary, and the sale of offices the secondary, channel of mobility. When after the outbreak of the Taiping rebellion the state began to lose its regulatory power, money overshadowed higher academic degrees as a determinant of social status.

In comparing social stratification in Ming-Ch'ing China with that of the early modern and modern West, we find that the difference is one of degree, not of kind. The demarcation between manual workers and those who labored with their minds may have been sharper in Confucian China than in the West, but such demarcation is found in practically all pre-modern and modern literate societies. Even in contemporary North America, which has a minimum of prejudice against manual work, one of the fundamental distinctions in the stratification system is that between white-collar and manual-labor occupations. Confucian tradition and values may have exerted greater pressure on the wealthy to gain entry into the ruling elite, but similar urges and social inferiority complexes are found in the *nouveaux riches* of most pre-modern and modern societies. Education, or more precisely a university degree, is becoming increasingly important in the stratification of the most "materialistic" North American societies. Even the meticulous legal regulations of the styles of life of various social classes in traditional China are not unique; they are shared by medieval and some postfeudal European societies. What is unusual about Ming-Ch'ing society is the overwhelming power of the bureaucracy and the ability of the state, in all but the last sixty years of a five and a half century period, to regulate the major channels of social mobility more or less in accordance with a time-honored guiding principle.

7

THE ART OF GOVERNMENT IN CHINA

E. A. Kracke, Jr.

In every dynasty realization of good government and dynastic survival itself called for a careful balancing of power among the persons and organs through whom the emperor acted. Isolated by stately pomp within his moated palace, the ruler retained practical freedom of action only through access to varied advice, independent sources of information, and officials of differing interests. Political progress was won through this lesson; the Han and the T'ang fell in learning it and the Ming through ignoring it. Emperors had to exclude from important functions their family and relatives by marriage, who were always prone to intrigue for influence and control of the succession to the throne, and equally the palace eunuchs, so favourably placed to monopolize access to the emperor's person. Within the bureaucracy itself power was divided through balances of several kinds. The highest direction of policy was confided to a Council of State, whose members were heads of several agencies. The Council's views and actions were scrutinized by separate organs of criticism. During the later T'ang and the Sung the emperor could consult also academies of distinguished scholars appointed to provide still another source of advice. To maintain the effectiveness of these structural checks and balances, it was imperative to guard vigilantly against domination of the several policy bodies by any

From "The Chinese and the Art of Government" by E. A. Kracke, Jr., in *The Legacy of China,* edited by Raymond Dawson (Oxford: The Clarendon Press, 1964), pp. 317–32. Excerpted and reprinted by permission of the publisher. Footnotes have been deleted.

faction or too like-minded a group. (Reformers rarely saw themselves as such a group, and since checks and balances came from the non-Confucian side of the tradition they were less honoured by theorists than they deserved to be.)

The principle of balance was reflected also in collegial organization of the various ministries and other central agencies, commonly headed by two officials similar in rank and authority. In provincial and local government and in military command it was obviously necessary to confide responsibility for a given function in a given area to a single official, but even here structural checks were provided. Under the Sung, the sharing of civilian functions on the provincial level by several intendants provided a degree of mutual surveillance. . . .

A special problem in China was the relation between policy-forming and executive action. Conceptually, policy was determined not by a preponderance of opinion but by a rational consensus achieved through objective discussion. Both policy suggestions and factual reports often originated with local officials, who were best informed on public needs, and passed through administrative channels to the Imperial Court. Since the Confucian ethos made each official personally responsible for popular welfare and criticism of government, officials at all levels ardently advocated one policy or another. Once policy was decided, each official had the duty of carrying it out in complete and meticulous conformity with the ruler's intention. Here came the difficulty. When an official's opinion conflicted with his duty as obedient executor, his actions and his reports might fall short of the needful co-operative zeal. Habits of over-independence thus justified could encourage a slackness that was likely enough in any case.

The difficulties of control implicit in Confucian responsibility perhaps helped to evoke the remarkable complex of organs for investigation, criticism, advice, and complaint, the perfecting of which took sixteen centuries. The primary organ of independent control was the Censorate, which acted in several ways to maintain proper functioning and health in all parts of the government. Its earliest duty was that of simple investigation, developed under the Ch'in as a natural authoritarian device. With the change of political philosophy in the Han this duty gained new implications. It came to mean not only spying out sedition and indiscipline, but also discovering inadequacies in the provision for public welfare in general. . . . Some time after the Han, devices for receiving popular petitions, inspired by early legend, were translated into reality and also further developed in the T'ang. Conspicuous among these devices were drums placed before the Imperial Palaces, to be struck by any man with a grievance, and slotted petition boxes which could be opened only by authorized officials. Under the Sung these simple practices were elaborated to provide a group of three complaint offices, administered by the Censorate. Reported users of the petition offices were primarily commoners. Complaints of the illiterate were written for them, and those who felt slighted could appeal to the second office and the third. The Mongols under Kublai Khan reinforced their control by heavy reliance on the Censorate in local administration. . . .

Still more significant was the censorial duty of criticizing the policies and actions of imperial ministers and the emperor himself. Such criticism, found already in the Han, expressed explicit Confucian doctrine, and grew without marked encouragement from the criticized. The moral position of the critic was hard to challenge, and his right to criticize with impunity won a secure place in the tradition. To strengthen censorial freedom from inhibiting pressures, T'ang practice provided that any censor could act without the permission of even the Censorate's chiefs. The censors were carefully removed from direct involvement in administration, and their action usually extended only to reports, accusations, or the initiation of judicial action, the judgement of which rested in other hands. They need not name the sources of their information. Officials responsible for criticizing policy were also appointed in other parts of the government, and a special officer was empowered to return for reconsideration even edicts bearing imperial approval. The height of critical effectiveness was reached in the eleventh century, when we are told that attacks by the critics agitated even emperors and brought down councillors of state. But censorial courage was still more remarkable in later dynasties when sharp criticism of rulers persisted—as in late Ming times—despite the occasional punishment or even execution of censors. The longevity of China's political system must be credited in significant degree to the power and vigilance of the Censorate.

Many less dramatic aspects of the system must also share credit. Innumerable minutiae of practice and organization added to administrative efficiency, many of them tracing back to the Han and being well developed by the T'ang and Sung. Precision and consistency of action were furthered by habits of conducting business in writing and recording actions carefully (often in duplicate). Objectivity and impartiality gained from the secrecy of ministerial deliberations and the publication of policy decisions and rules of operation. In the central administration the rather haphazard division of duties among early Han offices evolved by the T'ang into a more logical structure, and in the early eleventh century the many specialized bureaux came under three major departments responsible for general, economic, and military matters. In local administration, impelled by multiplying functions and aided by improved communications, the older division of authority by region and locality was modified to one whereby the offices at the capital—especially those with economic concerns—more often maintained direct contact with corresponding agencies on the local level. . . .

Most important among administrative methods were those concerned with personnel. Since the ruler depended on professional bureaucrats alike in the formation, implementation, and enforcement of policy, his success was proportional to bureaucratic ability and morale. Personnel policies assumed a major place in state deliberations. We have seen that early Chinese political thinkers evolved interesting concepts in this field; it is not too surprising that China was the first to develop many essential techniques. The primary aim was to improve the civil service proper, an élite group commonly numbering in the developed system some ten thousand or more and filling the key positions of central and local government. To obtain more and better men the emperor Wu of the Han founded a school at the capital which grew into a thriving university. Succeeding dynasties added local schools in all parts of the empire to train promising sons of official or commoner families at state expense.

Men were selected for government employment and advanced in

office through varied methods; from the T'ang onwards promotion and recruitment procedures were distinct. Rather primitive methods familiar elsewhere—nomination of officials' younger relatives and the sale of office—were gradually restricted and in later dynasties assumed importance only at moments of dynastic decline. In their place more constructive methods such as competitive examination, controlled sponsorship, and regular merit ratings came to play leading roles.

The earliest to develop was sponsorship. No method suited Confucian reform concepts so well as presentation of good men to the ruler by those in a position to judge their character. Tradition asserted that even in feudal times the public recommendation of such men for official position was an act of high merit, and their employment was pleasing to Heaven. By the Han at least the moral obligation assumed by the sponsor was supplemented by a legal responsibility for the acts of his protégé, and the system was widely employed to find men most highly qualified for government service. After the Han, however, recruitment through sponsorship became more and more restricted to rare instances in which exceptionally talented men had failed to seek advancement through normal channels. . . .

The examination system, which grew from sponsorship, was destined to occupy a greater place in the history of political institutions. This system served to select men for governmental service through regular written, competitive examinations, open to all candidates of good character, however they came by their training. The system was long in evolving. The earliest applications of examination technique are obscure. At least as early as 165 B.C. men recommended for office were required to answer in writing questions set by the Han emperor Wen. The emperor Wu followed this procedure regularly, placing the candidates in exact order of demonstrated merit. Han state university students were also promoted through written tests. In the early T'ang, competitive written examination of recommended men still produced on average less than ten graduates a year. At the end of the seventh century the empress Wu, usurping power and scheming to found a new dynasty, made competitive examination a tool to recruit supporters from the largely untapped talent of south-east China, and during successive years the number of degrees reached six times or more the earlier average. The T'ang emperor Hsüan-tsung, retrieving the throne, improved and strengthened his government with a series of measures; and examinations grew still more important. The number of graduates diminished with T'ang decline, but Sung rule revived the trend and in the eleventh century the annual average of final degrees passed two hundred and fifty. . . . The graduates could now supply the greater share of civil service posts.

With growing reliance on examination came contrivance of better methods. The chief of these were in use soon after A.D. 1000. Preliminary local tests and two tests at the capital eliminated some ninety-nine per cent of the contenders. Those who graduated were classed and numbered in order of ability. All would first hold rather minor offices, but examination ranking went far to determine subsequent promotions. Each examination paper was graded by three independent readers. Fair and objective reading was furthered by concealment of candidates' identities. A number replaced a candidates' name on his paper, which was copied out by clerks lest his handwriting be recognized. . . .

No one kind of test was felt to be fully adequate. Simple textual familiarity with the Classics did not prove intelligence. Answers to questions on meaning might, with effort enough, be learned by rote. Questions that called for an application of knowledge to conflicts of principle or administrative quandaries might evoke original thinking, but who could grade the answers accurately and objectively? Required compositions on prescribed topics in strictly formulated literary forms might show originality and ability, and could be graded more objectively, but did the studies they encouraged produce the most practical officials? Tests of these many kinds were multiplied and tried in varying versions and combinations. A single examination might last through several day-long sessions. But when any pattern of tests was long in use, clever tutors and assiduous study of past examinations could anticipate questions and supply formulas for glib answers. The best of forms had to change. Some critics decried all forms of written test as lacking the prime requisite —detection of character. . . .

We saw the high place accorded public welfare, both in theory and in administrative measures. How well was it furthered in practice? The answer of course varies according to the period. Morale and honesty naturally declined when dynasties weakened. The upper ranks of officialdom, normally selected for scholarship and character, at times lacked vigour and wisdom; except in times of eunuch influence they were rarely corrupt. On lower levels, salaries grew inadequate in difficult times, and clerical employees, selected more casually, had poorer *esprit de corps*. When good men supervised them, things went well, as popular petitions to retain such men in office demonstrated. At other times conditions were less happy. Laws were administered according to a carefully formulated code, revised in each dynasty. Legal concepts differed in several respects from those to which we are accustomed. Confucian theory, distrusting laws and advocating persuasion, discouraged litigation and urged the settlement of disputes through voluntary agreement, in which the local official often played a role. Problems of social or business relationship that in Western law might be settled by civil litigation were, when brought to court, often governed by laws of conduct enforced by penalties. Still extremely severe in the Han, the punishments were gradually lightened in later dynasties, those of physical mutilation being largely eliminated and capital crimes greatly reduced in number. Exile, forced labour, and the rod remained, but they were often commuted to fines varying according to a fixed schedule. Legal administration sought a justice that fitted the circumstances of each case. Where no irremediable damage had been done, the law provided that confession in advance of accusation should bring a lightened penalty or pardon. Offences were graver when the offended was one, such as a family elder, or official superior, who should command a special respect from the offender. Effort was made also to consider special extenuating circumstances. This called for a broad discretion on the part of the judge. Important cases were, however, regularly reviewed by higher judicial officials, the gravest receiving careful study by high courts at the capital.

How did the individual Chinese citizen fare in actuality? By what standards shall we measure the performance of government in practice, the justice of civil order achieved, the sum of individual freedom and contentment? Today we expect from government a standard made possible through long technical advances and the pooled political experience of the past. Perhaps the most relevant measure of China's success in earlier ages is that of the total impressions made on foreign witnesses, judging in terms of the Europe or the Near East of their times. Such witnesses often criticized certain practices and customs. But their praise of China's polity was almost universal. Arabs remarked the prevalence of literacy among all classes, and the honouring of business obligations. Marco Polo says of the last Sung ruler, whose Mongol successor he served:

> He loved peace and strictly maintained his kingdom in so great justice that none was found there who did evil or theft to any there, and the city was so safe that the doors of the houses and shops and stores full of all very dear merchandise often stayed open at night as by day and nothing at all was found missing there. For one could go freely through the whole kingdom safe and unmolested by night also as by day. It would be impossible to tell of the great wealth and the very great goodness which is in this kingdom so that the king was loved by all with very great reason.

Some three centuries later the Jesuit Ricci comments, as a good Christian, that

> every public office is therefore fortified with and dependent on the attested science, prudence, and diplomacy of the person assigned to it, whether he be taking office for the first time or is already experienced in the conduct of civil life. This integrity of life is prescribed by the law of [the Ming founder] Humvu, and for the most part it is lived up to, save in the case of such as are prone to violate the dictates of justice from human weakness and from lack of religious training among the gentiles.

By pre-modern Islamic and European political standards, it would seem that China did well.

8

LOCAL GOVERNMENT IN CHINA BEFORE MODERNIZATION

T'ung-tsu Ch'ü

At the beginning of this book I made the point that local government in China under the Ch'ing was highly centralized. The Chinese system, with the government of the various subdivisions of a province, down to the chou and hsien, under the control of the central government and administered by officials appointed by it, was parallel to the French system, where the prefect is directly responsible to the central government. But China had no local autonomy corresponding to that of the French communes. There was no government or council in the towns or villages, either in name or in fact. In this sense, the Chinese local government was even more centralized than the French.

The magistrate, who was under the supervision of officials at higher levels, was not empowered to make major decisions. Excepting in certain routine matters like the handling of minor civil cases, which were under his jurisdiction, the magistrate had to report to his superior and secure approval on most details of administration. This situation led Ku Yen-wu to conclude that "the magistrates possessed the least power among all officials."

Local government under the Ch'ing was ruled by an administrative code that was very comprehensive and apparently aimed at uniformity, rationality, precision, conformity, and centralization.

From *Local Government in China Under the Ch'ing* by T'ung-tsu Ch'ü (Cambridge, Mass.: Harvard University Press, 1962), pp. 193–99. Footnotes have been deleted.

But, paradoxically, these regulations also created technical difficulties and were inefficient. First, they were too rigid to allow the magistrate to exercise personal judgment or initiative. Second, the code made little allowance for regional differences, thus preventing the magistrate from adjusting administration to any special conditions in a locality.

It has been said that conformity is the universal value observed by all bureaucrats and often becomes an end in itself. Bureaucrats everywhere are disciplined to conform to the rules by a system of reward and punishment, which produces in the officials an attitude of timidity and an overconcern with conformity per se. In China this was carried to the extreme, for the administrative regulations were extraordinarily numerous and infractions always incurred punishment. Moreover, as we recall, for violating certain regulations, Chinese officials could not only be demoted or dismissed from office but could also be subjected to corporal punishment. This means that Chinese officials were liable to more severe punishment than are their counterparts in countries where a distinction is made between punishment for an administrative fault and for a criminal offense. In this situation it is to be expected that the main concern of most officials was to avoid punishment. This became even more accentuated because magistrates relied on their private secretaries in the conduct of local administration. The secretaries, being personally employed by the magistrate, felt obliged to avoid anything that would jeopardize the careers of their employers. Their guiding principle was apparently that strict adherence to regulations was the safest policy.

Yet at the same time we find that many laws and regulations were not actually in operation and had become more or less a formality. This occurred in almost every aspect of administration—for example, in relation to the term of service for the clerks and runners, and in the matter of customary fees. However, this did not mean that the officials and their aides could act entirely according to their own will. If the formal regulations governing some procedure were not operative, they had to follow the established custom. Any change from the established custom was likely to be resisted by the people. Thus the entire yamen staff developed a code of behavior acceptable both to themselves and to the local populace.

Local finance was also highly centralized, at least in theory. Officials of the local government, from the province down to the chou or hsien, acted only as agents of the central government in collecting and delivering taxes in accordance with the quotas set by the central government. They were not allowed to levy any taxes except likin, the local transit tax introduced in 1853. The local government thus had no revenue of its own, and even its operating budget was determined by the central government. No portion of the centrally administered taxes was allocated for local expenditure, with the exception of some limited items like the nominal salaries for officials, wages for runners, and sacrificial expenses. Nor was the local government allowed to add a centime to any national tax for local purposes. Consequently the local government was not provided with funds to meet the expenditures of local administration, including the collection and delivery of taxes to the central government.

This situation gave rise to the "customary fees" from which local government at various levels derived its revenue. Thus, while local finance was intended to be highly centralized, in practice it was decentralized. The fee system had no fixed rates, so the local officials had almost complete freedom in collecting and spending the fees. No distinction was made between yamen expenses and the personal expenses of the magistrate. The higher provincial officials had no control over the fees; they merely took their share of them.

From the data presented in the preceding chapters we may conclude that throughout the Ch'ing dynasty there was an over-all continuity in local administration, despite periodic revision of administrative regulations and formulation of new ones, all documented in great detail in the *Ch'ing hu-tien shih-li* (Collected statutes and cases of the Ch'ing dynasty). Most of these changes were technical and procedural and not very significant, particularly at the chou and hsien level. The organization of the yamen, its personnel, and their functions, and the pattern of supervision and of local finance all remained basically the same.

As we have seen, the functions of the local government were very comprehensive, the most important among them being tax collection and the administration of justice. In the sense that all these functions were under the magistrate's charge, he was a "one-man government," while his subordinate officials played a markedly insignificant role. Between the magistrate and his four groups of aides—clerks, runners, personal servants, and private secretaries—there was no intermediate authority; all were directly responsible to the magistrate.

The clerks, personal servants, and private secretaries all played an important part in local administration. But the role of the secretaries, who were the real administrative experts, was most significant. They were the nerve center of the yamen. The popular notion that Chinese bureaucracy was run by "amateurs" should be somewhat offset by the "expertness" of the magistrate's private secretaries, whose professional qualifications and experience were well recognized.

The magistrate stood in two distinct relationships to his aides. The clerks and runners, being natives and employed by the government, maintained a formal and impersonal relationship with the magistrate. The secretaries and personal servants were usually not natives; they were employed by the magistrate himself and were not considered government employees. Thus they maintained an informal and personal relationship with the magistrate.

As bureaucracy is characterized by a rational structure based on formal and impersonal relationships, the presence of informal and personal relationships in a government is often considered a hindrance to efficiency. However, the case of China seems to suggest that these elements have to be re-examined against a particular bureaucratic structure. The employment by the magistrate of aides with whom he maintained an informal and personal relationship may be viewed as a device to check and supervise the formal and impersonal group, whose efficiency depended upon such supervision. It should be kept in mind that, despite the informal and personal arrangement between the magistrate and his private secretaries, their employment was based primarily upon technical qualifications—competence and achievement. And in the discharge of their duties, they were mainly guided by administrative rules. Although they were not entirely free from consideration for their employer's professional security, their actions still had to be based on objective and calculable rules. Hence the "irrational" elements in local administration were reduced to a minimum.

Recent studies on industrial workers and military personnel have indicated the importance of the informal primary group in raising output and morale. Such findings show that "the human, the interpersonal, the informal factors," which have been generally ignored by students of the traditional science of public administration and bureaucracy, including Max Weber, "are of crucial administrative consequence." The private secretaries and personal servants of the magistrates seem to provide another example of how the informal and personal factors may operate within a formal structure to reduce administrative strain and gain greater efficiency. From this vantage point, supported by recent findings in the science of human relations in the West, one might well question the validity of the common notion that personal and informal relations are *always* incompatible with bureaucratic efficiency. The point is that efficiency cannot be examined superficially, merely in terms of personal versus impersonal and formal versus informal relations. We must also take into account other factors—criteria of eligibility, method of selection, terms of employment, and the like. Our data indicate that such factors had a profound influence on the behavior of all groups in the yamen.

Specifically, the superior status, pecuniary reward, and other attractions of a private secretaryship provided incentives for capable persons to embark on that career. Conversely, the lack of such attractions in the jobs of the clerks, runners, and personal servants made them unappealing to persons who could find better employment. Usually the opportunity for extralegal income was the chief motive in taking jobs that were otherwise so unrewarding. . . .

In sociological terms, the deviant behavior (from the point of view of morality and law) of the clerks, runners, and servants was largely a consequence of the dissociation of cultural values and social position. In other words, when one has no legitimate means to secure the desired values—pecuniary reward, career opportunity—owing to one's unprivileged position, one tends to seek these values by illegitimate means. To be sure, such dissociation occurs among all other unprivileged groups in society. But the crucial point here is that the personnel attached to a yamen not only had access to the illegitimate means but in fact also had immunity from prosecution, despite the formal regulations. "Accessibility with immunity" is an invitation to deviant behavior. Moreover, if the majority of the members of an occupation are engaged in deviant behavior, it is likely that they will exert pressure on the remaining members by demanding conformity. Nonconformity on the part of some members may cause group sanction in varying degrees. Thus what the government and the public consider deviant behavior or corruption may be regarded as conformity to the occupationally defined norms of behavior.

The inefficiency of the Chinese local government was largely due to poor organization and lack of coordination. One manifestation was the duplication of duties among the secretaries, clerks, and personal servants. The government policy of isolating personnel—that is, allowing them no opportunity for contact with one another—as a means of control made effective supervision difficult. Another source of inefficiency was the policy of not permitting private secretaries to participate in direct observation or investigation, a policy which resulted in judgments based on documents and other indirect sources of information.

With regard to the gentry, we have identified them as the local elite whose right to represent the local community was recognized by both the government and the public. They served as intermediary between the local officials and the people, gave advice to the former, and frequently took an active part in certain aspects of local administration. As participation of the local community in the administration of local affairs has often been considered a condition of local self-government, it is logical to ask whether the gentry's participation meant local self-government.

The answer to this question is no. In the first place, participation was limited to the gentry as a minority group. Second, the gentry were neither elected by the local people as their representatives nor appointed by the government as such. They were accepted as spokesmen for the community by dint of their privileged status. But their participation in government and their right to speak on behalf of the community were not formally defined, as in the case of an elected council in the West. There were no rules as to which gentry members should be consulted or invited to take part in administrative affairs. This was left largely to the local officials. Although the gentry might, and frequently did, intervene, there was no legal procedure whereby they might challenge or reject decisions made by the officials. In fact, the gentry's intervention took place mainly on a personal basis, and its effectiveness depended largely on the influence commanded by a particular member.

While the gentry could represent their own interests to the local government, there was no agent to represent other groups in the community. At most, the gentry were likely to be concerned with the welfare of the people only in the interest of general stability in the community. However, the gentry had no legal or political responsibility to protect the people. Any obligation they had was primarily moral and was carried out largely on a voluntary and informal basis. Furthermore, as a privileged group, the gentry's interests were at times in conflict with those of the rest of the community. This fact is again incompatible with self-government, which requires that the interests of the community as a whole be represented.

The gentry enjoyed status and privileges similar to those of the officials. Although the officials were linked with formal power and the gentry with informal power, the power of both groups derived from the political order. Only persons having such a politically determined status had access to the local officials and could have a voice in local policy. Thus the gentry was the only pressure group. They and the local officials together determined the local policy and administration and shared the control of society. As power means participation in the governing process or "participation in the making of decisions," we may conclude that local power in China under the Ch'ing was distributed only among the officials (formal government) and the gentry (informal government).

The action and interaction of all the groups we have studied in detail indicate that there were strains and tensions among them: between the magistrate and his superior officials, between the magistrate and the clerks, runners, and personal servants, between the officials and the local gentry, between the people and the officials and their subordinates, and between the people and the gentry. As strains and tensions are often stimuli to change, we naturally ask why they induced no noticeable change in the Chinese situation. A decisive factor, I suggest, is that all these groups, with the single exception of the common people, secured maximal returns under the existing system. Therefore, in spite of the tensions and conflicts among them, they were not interested in altering the *status quo,* and we find stability and continuity in the social and political order. This stability was threatened only when the dissatisfaction of the people was intense enough to culminate in open revolt. But so long as their dissatisfaction was not translated into effective action, the *status quo* was maintained.

9

PEASANT REBELLIONS IN CHINA

Yu-kung Kao

ECONOMIC AND POLITICAL PATTERNS

Overpopulation

It goes without saying that a peasant depends for his livelihood on the production of his land. If, for the moment, we set aside the peasant's relationship with the central administration and his landlord, four factors determine his living conditions, sometimes even his chances of survival: the amount of his land, the size of his family, weather and natural calamities, fertilization and irrigation of his land.

The amount of arable land in China did not materially increase, but population grew rapidly during long periods of peace. Therefore, with the practice of divided inheritance, the size of the Chinese peasant's arable land dwindled even without the contributing factors of land concentration and heavy taxation. Furthermore, the shortage of arable land might at any time be drastically aggravated by unpredictable natural calamities or by serious neglect of the irrigation systems which were chiefly maintained by the local government.

In such times of trouble, infanticide was one solution, rebellion was another. Chiang Meng-lin points out that except for the intro-

From "The Fang La Rebellion" by Yu-kung Kao, *Harvard Journal of Asiatic Studies* 24 (1962–63): 19–27. Reprinted by permission of the Harvard-Yenching Institute. Footnotes have been deleted.

duction of a new method of cultivation or expansion of irrigation to increase productivity and temporarily relieve overpopulation, population expansion eventually led to wars in which large numbers of people were eliminated. The reduction in population assured sufficient land for the peasantry and several decades of prosperity. This application of Malthus' theory to the Chinese scene seems to be valid. The problem of overpopulation was present during all of the major rebellions with the exception of those at the end of the Western Chin early in the fourth century A.D. when population had already been decreased by a long period of civil war.

Government Exactions

A peasant with a small plot of land and a large family, the pattern of most peasant households in China, could barely provide a living for his household even in a productive year, but the government still demanded the lion's share of this lean profit. At the beginning of a dynasty, far-sighted emperors such as Han Kao-tsu and T'ang T'ai-tsung usually tried to reduce taxation; consequently, many prosperous reigns came early in the dynasty. Near the end of a dynasty, the increase in government expenditure as a natural consequence of an expanding bureaucracy, the corruption of high officials and eunuchs, and the squanderings of extravagant emperors required ever higher taxes.

In addition to taxation, a farmer was regularly ordered to work for the government a certain number of days in the year as unpaid corvée. This practice of taking farmers from the fields was more of a burden than high taxation, especially when the work was on construction projects far from home. Evidence of high taxes and excessive corvée duty was in fact present in almost all early stages of rebellion and was usually claimed to be the direct cause of an uprising. Most notable cases are the rebellions against Ch'in Shih-huang-ti and Sui Yang-ti, both emperors who levied heavy taxes and engaged in extensive construction projects.

Land Concentration

Heavy taxes and one or two bad crops would quickly force the farmer to borrow from the usurer. Frequently when his debt could not be paid, a new debt was contracted to meet the payment of interest, which sometimes equalled or surpassed the amount of the original loan. This interest accumulating year after year forced the farmer to sell his land and become a tenant at the mercy of the local landlord. Distribution of land tended to be more equitable at the beginning of a dynasty because the war of accession had not only decreased the population and dispossessed the former élite and landlord class but also because the new government often began by redistributing land in addition to reducing taxes. Toward the close of a dynasty, however, there occurred an acceleration of land concentration in the hands of the imperial family, influential officials, and rich families with government connections. These landowners inflicted heavy rents on tenants and practiced usury. At such times the tax load fell on the decreasing number of independent farmers, while the great landholders were often successful in avoiding the land tax. Hsüeh Nung-shan asserts that this cycle in its later stages was the primary cause of rebellion. Close study of all peasant rebellions, especially that of the Yellow Turbans and those at the end of the Ming, tends to support this theory, although land concentration can never be demonstrated as the sole cause.

Nationalization and redistribution of land was attempted many times before the eighth century. Among the masses, the theory of socioeconomic equality appeared as early as the Yellow Turban Rebellion (184–192 A.D.). After the An Lu-shan Rebellion, private ownership of land was officially recognized, and no further attempts at nationalization were made. Thereafter it was the common people who voiced egalitarian slogans. In both the Wang Hsiao-po Rebellion (993–994 A.D.) and the Chung Hsiang Rebellion (1130–1135 A.D.), it was they who advocated eliminating the discrimination between rich and poor and equalizing property. During the T'ai-p'ing Rebellion (1850–1864), the rebel government developed an elaborate system of land distribution.

Monopoly

Brinton concludes from the study of four Western revolutions that among the economic motives of discontent, "the actual misery of certain groups in a given society" is much less important than "the existence among a group, or groups, of a feeling that prevailing conditions limit or hinder their economic activity." This observation, derived from evidence in more economically progressive societies, was, of course, not intended to apply to Chinese society. But we find that the merchants who competed with a government monopoly often cherished a similar resentment against authority's limiting their profits. The most important trades such as the production of salt, iron, wine, and tea were frequently seized by the government as monopolies, a policy which raised the price of the product to an exorbitant height and consequently invited smuggling.

Gradually smuggling itself became an important and profitable business, attracting adventurers, who sometimes carried on their operations with armed force. Therefore the establishment, change in policy, or strict enforcement of a monopoly would deprive hundreds of people of work or take away the profits of many others. Such groups, feeling that their means of livelihood had been unjustly removed, often resorted to banditry. Consumers who had to buy expensive salt or tea swallowed their resentment, but those who had formerly made a profit from the commodity revolted against the monopoly. Huang Ch'ao, who revolted in 874 A.D., was a salt smuggler, as were many of the leaders of the Fang La Rebellion and of the rebellions which occurred at the end of the Yüan.

Official Corruption

Popular grievance against a corrupt government was not limited to excessive taxation; three forms of corruption among officials at all levels spurred resentment in the people: the special privilege of tax exemption and official protection, the practice of taking bribes and imposing extra levies for private purposes, and a luxurious mode of life in contrast with peasant poverty. The typical picture of a corrupt administration was an extravagant or effete emperor, surrounded by greedy, corrupt, and infamous officials, relatives, and eunuchs, beneath whom swarmed dishonest and rapacious clerks. Under such a government, projects for public welfare were neglected, and any natural calamity could touch off an uprising. S. Y. Teng has called such political corruption the main cause of rebellion and has collected strong evidence to support his thesis.

Alienation of intellectuals, according to Brinton, was another preliminary sign of certain European revolutions. This symptom, however, is not completely applicable in the case of China where rebellion was usually preceded by the struggle of two rival factions at court. When, as often happened, the faction motivated by a desire for personal power and gain won out, the honest officials of the opposing faction were excluded from the government and exiled. Since these were the officials who usually enjoyed a good reputation in the local administrations where they served, the people's hope for better government was limited to the drastic alternative of revolt. Factional strife in the government before the Yellow Turban Rebellion and before the revolts at the end of the Ming are good examples.

Few intellectuals, however, allied themselves with rebel forces because of resentment toward a victorious rival faction. Confucian conditioning kept them loyal to the emperor under any circumstances, and their feeling of constituting a class superior to the masses prevented them from joining any peasant revolt in its early stages. When, however, such a revolt showed signs of gaining control of the whole realm, as in the case of Han Kao-tsu's and Ming T'ai-tsu's, the intellectuals in many instances offered their services to the peasant leaders.

IDEOLOGICAL PATTERNS

Unorthodox Religious Beliefs

Yuji Muramatsu has already examined this element of rebellion so thoroughly that one need but summarize his conclusions here. Supernatural beliefs prevailed in the mind of the Chinese peasant long before the introduction of Buddhism; and after the spread of Buddhism and Taoism among the masses, these primitive supernatural beliefs were further elaborated, developed, and incorporated into other religions.

The religions associated with popular rebellion had one or more of the following features in common:

a. Practicality. Such religions placed an emphasis on the problems of everyday life rather than on theological and philosophical problems. Although the adherents believed in a future life, they were more concerned with their immediate problems of economic distress and sickness.

b. Use of magic and sorcery. While these elements were used chiefly to awe congregations, they were also used in some cases for ritual healing.

c. Official proscription. Prohibition by the government increased the popularity of such religions with discontented people, who for the most part sought some faith which held out the promise not only of future happiness but of immediate enjoyment by changing the present world.

d. Communal organization. Strict discipline, regular contributions, and fraternal co-operation were characteristic of the social organization of congregations. Mutual help among members mitigated the economic difficulty of their lives. Asceticism was also encouraged.

e. Novelty. Often a new religion or one containing certain new elements gave the people an outlook different from the orthodox religions which had already disappointed them.

The various Taoist beliefs of the Yellow Turban Rebellion and Chang Hsiu's Rebellion of the same period, the Manichaeism of the Fang La Rebellion, and the role of the White Lotus Society in the rebellions at the end of the Yüan, are outstanding instances of the affinity between rebellion and unorthodox religion.

Nationalism

Nationalism did not play an important part in Chinese peasant uprisings until the rebellions at the end of the Yüan. During the Western Chin, Wang Mi's group allied with Hsiung-nu troops to plunder the capital. Fang La hoped to take advantage of the state of war between the Sung and the Liao to further his aims. Although many bandits, including some so-called Red Turban Armies, were active in North China against the Chin troops, Chung Hsiang revolted at the same time to harass the Sung government, which had just fled to the South. This is not to say that Chinese peasants had no hostility against barbarians; they acted without consideration of national security simply because they felt the government was a more immediate threat to their existence. Not many large-scale demonstrations of popular nationalism opposed the invasion of the Mongols and Manchus but it was a strong force in the rebellions at the end of the Yüan and during the T'ai-p'ing Rebellion.

The discontent of minority groups was seldom a factor in pre-Ch'ing rebellions, except at the end of the Western Chin when the new class of vagrants, dissatisfied with their ill-treatment, revolted under Chang Ch'ang in Hupei and under Wang Mi in Shantung. During Ming times there were also minor slave uprisings.

REBEL LEADERSHIP

Since the causes for rebellion among the masses and the motivation of rebel leaders were not always the same, a separate discussion of the social background, special qualifications, and motives of these leaders seems called for.

The traditional analysis of Chinese society finds two basic groups: the ruling class, including the emperor, his officials, and rich landowners, and the common people, including peasants, petty merchants, and artisans. Rich merchants and landowners were usually on good terms with the officials and collaborated both politically and financially with the government on most issues, and therefore can be classified as belonging to the ruling class.

Yuji Muramatsu, however, has pointed out that "between the two main strata of Chinese society, . . . there seems to have been a third or middle layer of literate but originally powerless intellectuals: monks, priests, jobless lower-degree holders, and the like, including such pseudo-intellectuals as fortunetellers and sorcerers." This third group, he continues, came partly from hermits of upper-class origin and partly from the more enterprising members of the lowest social classes.

A clear definition of this third class will help us to understand the structure of Chinese society in general and peasant rebellions in particular, since almost all rebel leaders came from its ranks. As a class it was made up of monks, priests or fortune-tellers, petty merchants, small landowners, smugglers, government clerks or servants, petty army officers, lower-degree holders, and tutors. Most of the people in these professions had risen through their enterprise from the lowest class but were unable to achieve any standing in the upper class.

Although, as Muramatsu suggests, there were "hermits" of upper-class origin—that is, members of the gentry who repudiated its civil obligations without, however, becoming social recluses—they were in spirit detached from the people.

This third class, then, was not a homogeneous one; and while most of its members were in general contented citizens, many cherished some grievance against the government which adverse conditions could aggravate into revolt. Petty merchants and small landowners were the most co-operative as long as the burden of taxation was bearable. Those who worked in local government offices or served in the army took a risky advantage of their position to make illegal profits. At the extreme of illegality were the smugglers, men of adventurous spirit who were tempted by the extent of government monopolies into a profitable criminal career and who operated in armed bands under military discipline. Monks and priests were submissive to authority when their religion was tolerated, but those who propagated unorthodox and officially proscribed religions were naturally hostile to the government. Lower-degree holders and tutors were, of course, frustrated scholars without family background; and though they may have complained of injustice at the examinations, they tended to remain loyal to the government because of the Confucian indoctrination of their studies.

The qualities which these groups had in common were that they were usually more intelligent, more experienced, or financially better off than the majority of the lowest class. Whenever a revolt was in the making, therefore, it was they to whom the people looked for leadership and it was they who took advantage of disturbed conditions to advance their own fortunes.

We may conclude, then, that no single factor alone stirred up a rebellion, although often, when the circumstances were ripe, a single cause may appear to have created the revolt. Among the many symptoms which foreshadow a rebellion, extreme economic pressure and ideological conflict are the most crucial. The personal ambition of the individual rebel leader is the unpredictable spark which may touch off the uprising and his capability is a major force in directing its future course.

10

BASIC CONCEPTS OF CHINESE LAW

Derk Bodde and Clarence Morris

SCOPE AND SIGNIFICANCE OF CHINESE LAW

Western scholars on China, with only a few distinguished exceptions, have until recently shown but little interest in the study of Chinese law. Today, especially in the United States, the situation is changing, but the stimulus obviously comes much more forcibly from the China of Mao Tse-tung than from the law of pre-Republican (pre-1912) China, which, especially in its formal codified aspects, is the subject of this [article].

Good reasons can of course be found to explain the traditional indifference. They include the lack of legal training or interest among all but a handful of earlier Western sinologists, the formidable difficulties in style and vocabulary of the Chinese legal literature, and the fact that Chinese scholars themselves usually regarded this literature as utilitarian only and hence as little worthy of study on esthetic or inspirational grounds.

Behind this last point, however, lie other more basic considerations: the fact that the written law of pre-modern China was overwhelmingly penal in emphasis, that it was limited in scope to being primarily a legal codification of the ethical norms long dominant in Chinese society, and that it was nevertheless rarely invoked to uphold these norms except when other less punitive measures had

From *Law in Imperial China* by Derk Bodde and Clarence Morris (Cambridge, Mass.: Harvard University Press, 1967), pp. 3–29. Copyright, 1967, by the President and Fellows of Harvard College. Reprinted by permission of the publisher. Footnotes have been deleted.

failed. Chinese traditional society, in short, was by no means a legally oriented society despite the fact that it produced a large and intellectually impressive body of codified law.

The penal emphasis of this law, for example, meant that matters of a civil nature were either ignored by it entirely (for example, contracts), or were given only limited treatment within its penal format (for example, property rights, inheritance, marriage). The law was only secondarily interested in defending the rights—especially the economic rights—of one individual or group against another individual or group and not at all in defending such rights against the state. What really concerned the law—though this is to be surmised rather than explicitly read in the Chinese legal literature—were all acts of moral or ritual impropriety or of criminal violence which seemed in Chinese eyes to be violations or disruptions of the total social order. The existence of the norms of propriety was intended to deter the commission of such acts, but once they occurred, the restoration of social harmony required that punishment be inflicted to exact retribution from their doer. In the final analysis, a disturbance of the social order really meant, in Chinese thinking, a violation of the total cosmic order because, according to the Chinese world-view, the spheres of man and nature were inextricably interwoven to form an unbroken continuum.

For these reasons, the official law always operated in a vertical direction from the state upon the individual, rather than on a horizontal plane directly between two individuals. If a dispute involved two individuals, individual A did not bring a suit directly against individual B. Rather he lodged his complaint with the authorities, who then decided whether or not to prosecute individual B. No private legal profession existed to help individuals plead their cases, and even in the government itself, because law was only the last of several corrective agencies, officials exclusively concerned with the law operated only on the higher administrative levels. On the lowest level, that of the *hsien* (district or county), which was the level where governmental law impinged most directly upon the people, its administration was conducted by the *hsien* magistrate as merely one of his several administrative functions. Although he usually lacked any formal legal training, he was obliged to act as detective, prosecutor, judge, and jury rolled into one.

Fortunately for the operation of the system, however, the magistrate was commonly assisted in his judicial work by a legal secretary who *did* possess specialized knowledge of the law, and who, on behalf of the magistrate, could prepare cases for trial, suggest appropriate sentences, or write the legal reports which went to higher governmental levels. Yet it is indicative of the Chinese attitude toward law that this secretary did not himself belong to the formal administrative system. He was merely a personal employee of the magistrate, who paid his salary out of his own private purse. Hence the secretary was not permitted to try cases himself or otherwise to take an active part in the trials. However, to avoid miscarriages of justice on this lowest administrative level, a very carefully defined system of appeals existed which automatically took all but minor cases to higher levels for final judgment—in the case of capital crimes as far upward as the emperor himself.

How law in imperial China became the embodiment of the ethical norms of Confucianism will be discussed later. Here it should be stressed that in China, perhaps even more than in most other civilizations, the ordinary man's awareness and acceptance of such norms was shaped far more by the pervasive influence of custom and the usages of propriety than by any formally enacted system of law. The clan into which he was born, the guild of which he might become a member, the group of gentry elders holding informal sway in his rural community—these and other extra-legal bodies helped to smooth the inevitable frictions in Chinese society by inculcating moral precepts upon their members, mediating disputes, or, if need arose, imposing disciplinary sanctions and penalties.

The workings of such unofficial agencies were complemented by procedures on the part of the government, procedures which, despite their official inspiration, functioned quite separately from the formal legal system. These extra-legal organs and procedures, then, were what the Chinese everyman normally looked to for guidance and sanction, rather than to the formal judicial per se. Involvement in the formal system was popularly regarded as a road to disaster and therefore to be avoided at all cost. "Win your lawsuit and lose your money," runs a Chinese proverb. Or again: "Of ten reasons by which a magistrate may decide a case, nine are unknown to the public."

One might conclude that the real reason for the Western neglect of Chinese formal law is that this law is not inherently deserving of much attention. Such a conclusion, however, would be unfortunate on several counts. In the first place, law is an important touchstone for measuring any civilization, and its differing role in China as compared with its role in the West points to basic societal differences between the two civilizations which deserve detailed analysis. In the second place, the various extra-legal bodies for social control mentioned above, despite their obvious importance and the generalized remarks about them to be found in many writings, are very difficult to study with precision because of their scattered and informal mode of operation, and the fact that what they did and said was often either not written down at all or, if written, not readily available in published form.

The literature on formal Chinese law, by contrast, is large in quantity, fairly readily available, and covers a longer time span than that of any other present-day political entity. It includes the legal sections in various encyclopedic compilations of governmental institutions, the chapters on legal development in many of the dynastic histories, several large compendia of actual law cases, and above all the voluminous law codes of successive dynasties. The codes, in particular, have a continuity and authoritativeness which make them unrivaled instruments for measuring precisely, dynasty by dynasty, the shifting configurations of Chinese social and political values as officially defined. So far this challenging task has hardly been attempted.

The most recent of the dynastic codes is that of the Ch'ing or Manchu dynasty (1644–1911). It was compiled in definitive form in 1740 and consists of 436 sections that contain a greater number of statutes and approximately 1,800 sub-statutes. For previous dynasties there also exists a sequence of earlier codes going back to the T'ang Code of 653, in 501 articles. Before this date, no codes survive save for scattered quotations in other works. However, a study still in progress has already yielded a wealth of information on the code and judicial procedure of the first lengthy imperial dynasty, that of Han (206 B.C.–A.D. 220).

Prior to the Han and its short-lived predecessor, the Ch'in dynasty (221–207 B.C.), no centralized empire yet existed in China. At that time there were only a number of independent and mutually warring principalities. This pre-imperial age, often called the age of Chinese feudalism because of its institutional similarities to medieval Europe, is also the age that saw the formative beginnings of Chinese written law. Excluding unreliable myth and legend, the earliest datable evidence of such written law is the promulgation in 536 B.C. of certain "books of punishment" in one of these principalities. . . .

THE EARLIEST CHINESE "CODE"

. . . The Chou dynasty (ca. 1027–221 B.C.) functioned during its early centuries under a political system which has often been compared to European feudalism. At the top were the Chou kings, who exercised nominal sovereignty over the entire Chinese cultural world. Under them were vassal lords who held as fiefs from the Chou house a multitude of small principalities, which were subdivided in turn into the estates of subordinate lords and officials. At the bottom of the pyramid came the peasant serfs, hereditarily attached to these estates. In the course of time, however, the vassal principalities broke away from the Chou overlordship and became completely independent states. By the sixth century B.C., a combination of social, political, economic, and technological forces was bringing about an accelerating dissolution of the old order.

The new forces included, among others: new agricultural techniques which made increases in population possible; the growth of commerce and rise of a money economy; the buying and selling of land and partial freeing of the peasants from their former serfdom; a growing administrative complexity in the state governments; and the appearance of competing schools of philosophy and politics. The final centuries of the Chou dynasty, appropriately known as the Period of the Warring States (403–221 B.C.), saw increasingly bitter warfare between the few large states still surviving, till one of them, the state of Ch'in, succeeded in swallowing up its rivals one by one, and in 221 B.C. finally created the first centralized empire in Chinese history.

Such is the background of interrelated changes against which should be viewed the creation of the first "codes" of written law in the late sixth century B.C. The earliest reliably known to us is the "books of punishment" (*hsing shu*) which Tzu-ch'an, prime minister of the state of Cheng, ordered to be inscribed in 536 B.C. on a set of bronze tripod vessels. His action was followed by similar steps in this and other states in 513, 501, and later. Although the texts of these "codes" have in every case been lost, we may judge of the opposition they aroused from the famed letter of protest which the high dignitary of a neighboring state, Shu-hsiang, sent to Tzu-ch'an upon the promulgation of the Cheng laws:

> Originally, sir, I had hope in you, but now that is all over. Anciently, the early kings conducted their administration by deliberating on matters [as they arose]; they did not put their punishments and penalties [into writing], fearing that this would create a contentiousness among the people which could not be checked. Therefore they used the principle of social rightness (*yi*) to keep the people in bounds, held them together through their administrative procedures, activated for them the accepted ways of behavior (*li*), maintained good faith (*hsin*) toward them, and presented them with [examples of] benevolence (*jen*) . . .
>
> But when the people know what the penalties are, they lose their fear of authority and acquire a contentiousness which causes them to make their appeal to the written words [of the penal laws], on the chance that this will bring them success [in court cases] . . . Today, sir, as prime minister of the state of Cheng, you have built dikes and canals, set up an administration which evokes criticism, and cast [bronze vessels inscribed with] books of punishment. Is it not going to be difficult to bring tranquility to the people in this way? . . . As soon as the people know the grounds on which to conduct disputation, they will reject the [unwritten] accepted ways of behavior (*li*) and make their appeal to the written word, arguing to the last over the tip of an awl or knife. Disorderly litigations will multiply and bribery will become current. By the end of your era, Cheng will be ruined. I have heard it said that a state which is about to perish is sure to have many governmental regulations.

To this criticism, Tzu-ch'an's brief reply was polite but uncompromising:

> As to your statements, sir, I have neither the talents nor ability to act for posterity. My object is to save the present age. Though I cannot accept your instructions, dare I forget your great kindness?

This letter is eloquent testimony to the unchanging spirit of conservatism throughout the ages. Shu-hsiang's criticisms of dike and canal building and of bigness in government are recognizably those of any conservative legislator today whenever he attacks public spending and demands a balanced budget. What is uniquely Chinese and therefore most significant about the letter, however, is its insistence upon the moral and political dangers involved in the public promulgation of legal norms. This view of law seems to have no real parallel in any other civilization.

It should not surprise us that Shu-hsiang's letter is strongly Confucian in tone, notably in its use of such Confucian terms as *yi, li, hsin* and *jen.* For though Confucius was but fifteen when the letter was written, these terms and the ideas they connoted were surely already "in the air" when he was young, and were not complete innovations with himself.

CONFUCIANS AND LEGALISTS

Although Shu-hsiang himself cannot be formally counted a Confucian, his letter nevertheless epitomizes what may be termed the "purist" Confucian view of law. As we shall see shortly, the Confucians were staunch upholders of the traditional "feudal" scale of values. Hence it is natural that they should be bitterly hostile to the new law, especially in its early stages. Later, however, as it became increasingly apparent that law had come to stay, the Confucians softened their attitude to the point where they accepted law—although grudgingly—as a necessary evil. Even then, however, they remained Confucian in their insistence that the public enacting of law is not necessary in the ideal state, and that even in the inferior administrations of their own times, government by law should always be kept secondary to government by moral precept and example.

Opposed to the Confucians were men who, because of their ardent advocacy of law, eventually came to be known as the Legalists or School of Law (*fa chia*). Most of them were less theoretical thinkers than tough-minded men of affairs who, as administrators, diplomats, and political economists, sought employment from whatever state would use their services. Their aim was direct and simple: to create a political and military apparatus powerful enough to suppress feudal privilege at home, expand the state's territories abroad, and eventually weld all the rival kingdoms into a single empire. Toward this goal they were ready to use every political, military, economic and diplomatic technique at their disposal. Their insistence on law, therefore, was motivated by no concern for "human rights," but simply by the realization that law was essential for effectively controlling the growing populations under their jurisdiction. In thinking and techniques they were genuine totalitarians, concerned with men in the mass, in contrast to the Confucians, for whom individual, family, or local community were of paramount importance. Yet it would be unfair to regard them merely as unscrupulous power-hungry politicians, for they sincerely believed that only through total methods could eventual peace and unity be brought to their war-torn world. If asked why they did what they did, they would no doubt have echoed Tzu-ch'an's dictum: "My object is to save the present age."

CONFUCIAN VIEWS OF *LI* AND LAW

As against the Legalists' *fa* or law, the key Confucian term is *li.* This word has an extraordinarily wide range of meanings. In its narrowest (and probably original) sense, it denotes the correct performance of all kinds of religious ritual: sacrificing to the ancestors at the right time and place and with the proper deportment and attitude is *li;* so is the proper performance of divination. In this sense *li* is often translated as ritual or rites. In a broader sense, however, *li* covers the entire gamut of ceremonial or polite behavior, secular as well as religious. There are numerous rules of *li* for all customary situations involving social relationships, such as receiving a guest, acquiring a wife, going into battle, and the many other varied duties and activities of polite society. In this sense, *li* is often translated as ceremonial, politeness, etiquette, or rules of proper conduct. Finally, *li* in its broadest sense is a designation for all the institutions and relationships, both political and social, which make for harmonious living in a Confucian society. The *li,* in short, constitute both the concrete institutions and the accepted modes of behavior in a civilized state.

The Confucians believed that the *li* had been created by the ancient sages, and that the disorder of their own age resulted from men's failure to understand or live according to these *li*. A prime Confucian duty, therefore, was to study and interpret the *li* as handed down from antiquity so as to make them meaningful for the present day. This idea led the Confucians to prepare several written compilations of *li* which, however, did not assume final form until near the end of the feudal age and during the early part of the age of empire. During most of the Chou dynasty, consequently, the *li* were transmitted in unwritten form only. At the same time, their large number, complexity, and refinement meant that they were largely an upper-class monopoly. Indeed, what most readily distinguished the Confucian ideal gentleman (the *chün-tzu* or Superior Man) from ordinary men was his mastery of the *li*.

On the other hand, the Confucians believed that underlying the minutiae of the specific rules of *li* are to be found certain broad moral principles which give the *li* their validity because they are rooted in innate human feeling; in other words, they represent what men in general instinctively feel to be right. It is this interpretation of *li* which has caused some modern scholars to suggest that a comparison may be made between Confucian *li* and the Western concept of natural law in apposition to a comparison between Legalist *fa* and Western positive law.

Finally, and this point is important, the early *li* were the product of a society in which hierarchical difference was emphasized. That is to say, the *li* prescribed sharply differing patterns of behavior according to a person's age and rank both within his family and in society at large (one pattern when acting toward a superior, another toward an inferior, still a third toward an equal). This idea of hierarchical difference, with resulting differences in behavior and privilege, has remained alive in Confucianism throughout imperial times, despite the disappearance of the pre-imperial feudal society that first gave it birth.

Following is a summary of the main Confucian argument with the Legalists from the point of view of a "purist" Confucian:

1. Man is by nature good (Mencius, 371?–289? B.C.), or at least is a rational being capable of learning goodness (Hsün Tzu, ca.

298–ca. 238 B.C.). It is by inculcating the *li* that society shapes the individual into a socially acceptable human being. The *li* are thus preventive in that they turn the individual away from evil before he has the chance of committing it, whereas law (*fa*) is punitive in that it only comes into action to punish the individual for evil already committed.

2. A government based on virtue can truly win the hearts of men; one based on force can only gain their outward submission. The *li* are suasive and hence the instrument of a virtuous government; laws are compulsive and hence the instrument of a tyrannical government.

3. The *li* derive their universal validity from the fact that they were created by the intelligent sages of antiquity in conformity with human nature and with the cosmic order. Law has no moral validity because it is merely the ad hoc creation of modern men who wish by means of it to generate political power.

4. The five major relationships of Confucianism—those of father and son, ruler and subject, husband and wife, elder and younger brother, friend and friend—are instinctive to man and essential for a stable social order. The *li* reinforce these and similar relationships by prescribing modes of behavior differing according to status, whereas law obliterates the relationships by imposing a forced uniformity.

5. The *li* (meaning at this point primarily rites and ceremony) give poetry and beauty to life. They provide channels for the expression of human emotion in ways that are socially acceptable. Law, on the contrary, is mechanistic and devoid of emotional content.

6. A government based on *li* functions harmoniously because the *li,* being unwritten, can be flexibly interpreted to meet the exigencies of any particular situation. A government based on law creates contention because its people, knowing in advance what the written law is, can find means to circumvent it, and will rest their sophistical arguments on the letter rather than the spirit of the law.

7. Laws are no better than the men who create and execute them. The moral training of the ruler and his officials counts for more than the devising of clever legal machinery.

To give the flavor of the Confucian spokesmen themselves, the following are offered as a few representative quotations. Included, however, are two of non-Confucian origin, illustrative of the fact that the Confucian distrust of law was shared by other schools of thought, though sometimes for different reasons:

> In hearing cases I am as good as anyone else, but what is really needed is to bring about that there are no cases!
>
> Lead the people by regulations, keep them in order by punishments (*hsing*), and they will flee from you and lose all self-respect. But lead them by virtue and keep them in order by established morality (*li*), and they will keep their self-respect and come to you.
>
> The more laws (*fa*) and ordinances (*ling*) are promulgated, the more thieves and robbers there will be.
>
> Goodness alone [without law] does not suffice for handling government. Law (*fa*) alone [without goodness] cannot succeed in operating of itself.
>
> To have good laws (*fa*) and yet experience disorder—examples of this have indeed existed. But to have a Superior Man (*chün-tzu*) and yet experience disorder—this is something which from antiquity until today has never been heard of.
>
> Laws (*fa*) cannot stand alone, and analogies cannot act of themselves. When they have the proper man, they survive; when they lack the proper man, they disappear. Law is the basis of good government, but the Superior Man (*chün-tzu*) is the origin of the law. Therefore when there is a Superior Man, the laws, though they may be numerically reduced, succeed in being all-pervading. When there is no Superior Man, the laws, though they may be all-embracing, lose their power of orderly enforcement, are unable to respond to the changes of affairs, and suffice only to bring confusion.
>
> The Legalists (*fa chia*) make no distinction between kindred and strangers, nor do they differentiate the noble from the humble. All such are judged by them as one before the law (*fa*), thereby sundering the kindliness expressed in affection toward kindred and respect toward the honorable. Their program might perhaps be followed a single time, but it is not one to be used for long. Hence I say of them that they are stern and deficient in kindliness.
>
> A good government is one that takes benevolence (*jen*) and social rightness (*yi*) as its basic roots, and laws (*fa*) and regulations (*tu*) as its lesser twigs . . . He who gives priority to the roots, but only secondary place to the twigs, is termed a Superior Man (*chün-tzu*),

whereas he who lets his concern for the twigs result in damage to the roots is termed a petty man (*hsiao jen*) . . . To ignore cultivation of the roots while devoting effort to the twigs is to neglect the trunk while giving water to the branches. Law, moreover, has its birth in the upholding of benevolence and social rightness, so that to lay great weight on law while discarding social rightness is to value one's cap and shoes while forgetting one's head and feet.

The rules of polite behavior (*li*) do not reach down to the common people; the punishments (*hsing*) do not reach up to the great dignitaries.

THE LEGALISTS AND LAW

The main arguments of the Legalist position are as follows:

1. Although a very few persons may be found who are naturally altruistic, the great majority of men act only out of self-interest. Therefore, stern punishments are necessary. Law is concerned only with the many who are selfish, not with the insignificant few who are good.

2. A government, if it is to be strong, must destroy factionalism and privilege. Hence it is imperative for it to publicize its laws to all and to apply them impartially to high and low alike, irrespective of relationship or rank.

3. Law is the basis of stable government because, being fixed and known to all, it provides an exact instrument with which to measure individual conduct. A government based on *li* cannot do this, since the *li* are unwritten, particularistic, and subject to arbitrary interpretation.

4. A vital principle for reducing particularism and thereby strengthening the state is that of group responsibility. Let the population be grouped into units of five or ten families each, and within each such unit let every individual be equally responsible for the wrongdoing of every other individual, and equally subject to punishment if he fails to inform the authorities of such wrongdoing.

5. Because history changes, human institutions must change accordingly. In antiquity people were few and life was easy, but today the growth of population has resulted in a sharpening

struggle for existence. Hence, the *li* of the ancients no longer fit modern conditions and should be replaced by a system of law. Law should certainly not be changed arbitrarily; yet if it is to retain its vitality it should equally certainly be kept ever responsive to the shifting needs of its time.

6. A state that is strong is one that maintains a single standard of morality and thought for its people. All private standards must be suppressed if they do not agree with the public standard as prescribed by law.

7. Men, being essentially selfish, cannot be induced merely by moral suasion to act altruistically. Only by playing on their own self-interest can the state induce them to do what it desires. Hence the wise ruler establishes a system of rewards and punishments in such a way that citizens—especially officials holding important positions—are rewarded if their performance accords exactly with the specific responsibilities attached to their position but punished when this performance either falls short or exceeds these specified responsibilities.

8. The importance of individual capabilities in government is lessened when there is good legal machinery. Thus even a mediocre ruler, provided he keeps to his laws, can have a good administration.

9. Laws that are sufficiently stringent will no longer have to be applied because their mere existence will be enough to deter wrongdoing. Thus harsh laws, though painful in their immediate effects, lead in the long run to an actual reduction of government and to a society free from conflict and oppression.

That the foregoing summary represents the Legalist position is supported by the following quotations:

For governing the people there is no permanent principle save that it is the laws (*fa*) and nothing else that determine the government. Let the laws roll with the times and there will be good government. Let the government accord with the age and there will be great achievement . . . But let the times shift without any alteration in the laws and there will be disorder. Let human capabilities multiply without any modification in the prohibitions and there will be territorial dismemberment. This is why, in the sage's governing of men, the laws shift with the times and the prohibitions vary with the capabilities.

If the law (*fa*) is not uniform, it will be inauspicious for the holder of the state . . . Therefore it is said that the law must be kept uniform. It is out of this that preservation or destruction, order or disorder, develop, and this it is that the sage-ruler uses as the great standard for the world . . . All beings and affairs, if not within the scope of the law, cannot operate . . . When ruler and minister, superior and inferior, noble and humble, all obey the law, this is called great good government.

What are mutually incompatible should not coexist. To reward those who kill the enemy, yet at the same time praise acts of mercy and benevolence; to honor those who capture cities, yet at the same time believe in the doctrine of universal love; to improve arms and armies as preparation against emergency, yet at the same time admire the flourishes of the officials at the court; to depend on agriculture to enrich the nation, yet at the same time encourage men of letters: . . . strong government will not thus be gained. The state in times of peace feeds the scholars and cavaliers, but when difficulty arises it makes use of its soldiers. Those whom it benefits are not those whom it uses, and those whom it uses are not those whom it benefits . . . What is today called wisdom consists of subtle and speculative theories which even the wisest have difficulty in understanding . . . Now in ordering current affairs, when the most urgent needs are not met, one should not concern oneself with what is of no immediate bearing . . . Therefore subtle and speculative theories are no business of the people.

In his rule of a state, the sage does not rely on men doing good of themselves, but uses them in such a way that they can do no wrong. Within the frontiers, those who can be relied on to do good of themselves are not enough to be counted in tens, whereas if men be used so as to do no wrong, the entire state may be equably administered. He who rules makes use of the many while disregarding the few, and hence he concerns himself not with virtue but with law (*fa*).

When punishments are heavy, the people dare not transgress, and therefore there will be no punishments.

When a ruler wishes to prevent wickedness, he examines into the correspondence between performance and title, words and work. When a minister makes claims, the ruler gives him work according to what he has claimed, but holds him wholly responsible for accomplishment corresponding to this work. When the accomplishment corresponds to the work, and the work corresponds to what the man has claimed he could do, he is rewarded. If the accomplishment does not correspond to the work, nor the work correspond to what the man has claimed for himself, he is punished. Thus when ministers have made great claims while their actual accomplishment is small, they are punished. This is not punishment because of the smallness of the accomplishment, but because the accomplishment is not equal to the name of it. And when ministers have made small claims while the actual accomplishment is great, they are also punished. This is not because no pleasure is taken in the larger accomplishment, but because it is not in accord with the name given to it.

In governing a state, the regulating of clear laws (*fa*) and establishing of severe punishments (*hsing*) are done in order to save the masses of the living from disorder, to get rid of calamities in the world, to insure that the strong do not override the weak and the many do not oppress the few, that the aged may complete their years and the young and orphaned may attain maturity, that the border regions not be invaded, that ruler and minister have mutual regard for each other and father and son mutually support one another, and that there be none of the calamities of death, destruction, bonds and captivity. Such indeed is the height of achievement.

LEGALIST TRIUMPH BUT CONFUCIANIZATION OF LAW

A reading of the Confucian and Legalist platforms should be enough to tell us what happened. The dynamic and ruthlessly efficient program of the Legalists, as adopted in Ch'in, helped that state to triumph successively over its rivals and in 221 B.C. to found the first universal Chinese empire. Under the new regime the nobles and officials of the former states were taken away from their territories and stripped of power. Their place was taken by a centrally appointed, nonhereditary, salaried bureaucracy which was to be the model for all dynastic governments from that time onward until the founding of the Republic in 1912. The Legalist law of Ch'in became the law of the entire empire. Finally, in 213 B.C., the Legalist program reached its logical climax with the notorious "Burning of the Books," expressly ordered by the government to destroy the classical texts of antiquity, the writings of the non-Legalist schools of thought, and the historical records of former states other than Ch'in.

Yet the Legalist triumph was amazingly short-lived. In 210 B.C. the founder of the Ch'in empire died, and within two years his empire dissolved into rebellion and disorder. Out of the subsequent civil war arose a new empire, that of Han (206 B.C.–A.D. 220), under which the Ch'in bureaucratic government was re-established and elaborated. At the same time, however, in one of the amazing reversals of history, Confucianism replaced Legalism as the dominant ideology. Already by 100 B.C. Confucianism was beginning to gain recognition as the orthodoxy of the state, whereas Legalism was disappearing for all time as a separate school.

However, the Confucianism which triumphed in Han times was a highly eclectic thought system—one that borrowed extensively from its philosophical rivals. Because these rivals included Legalism, the eclipse of Legalism as a recognized school by no means meant the complete disappearance of Legalist ideas and practices. On the contrary, Legalism continued to influence the political and economic thinking of Han and later times, probably a good deal more than has been traditionally supposed. Such economic policies, for example, as the "ever-normal granary," various government efforts to equalize private holdings of land, or governmental monopolies of salt, iron, and other products, all probably owe as much or more to Legalism than they do to early Confucianism. Recent study shows that the same may even be true of what has traditionally been thought to be a peculiarly Confucian institution: the civil service examination system used in imperial times to recruit government personnel on the basis of intellect rather than birth.

It would be strange, therefore, if Legalism did not leave a lasting mark on law. Its influence probably explains, for example, the continuing penal emphasis found in all the imperial codes, and the resulting fact that their treatment even of administrative and other noncriminal matters usually follows a standard formula: "Anyone who does x is to receive punishment y." Or again, the background of Legalism probably explains certain important features of imperial judicial procedure: the nonexistence of private lawyers; the assumption (nowhere explicitly stated but everywhere implied in the treatment of defendants) that a suspect must be guilty unless and until he is proven innocent; or the legal use of torture (within certain specified limits) for extracting confession from suspects who stubbornly refuse to admit guilt despite seemingly convincing evidence against them. Still another idea which probably owes much to Legalism is that of group responsibility (especially conspicuous in treason cases and the like). Here, however, Confucian emphasis on family and communal solidarity has probably also contributed considerably. The earliest roots of the concept, indeed, may well go back to an early communal stage of Chinese social thinking predating either Confucianism or Legalism.

Despite these and other probable survivals from Legalism, the really spectacular phenomenon of imperial times is what has been aptly termed the Confucianization of law—in other words, the incorporation of the spirit and sometimes of the actual provisions of the Confucian *li* into the legal codes. This process got under way during Han times only gradually and thereafter continued over several centuries. By the enactment of the T'ang Code in 653, however, it had effectively closed the one-time breach between *li* and *fa*. Customary morality (*li*) achieved official status in the form of positive law (*fa*), or, to reverse the equation and use another scholar's interpretation . . . positive law (*fa*) achieved moral status as the embodiment of natural law (*li*). As T'ung-tsu Ch'ü rightly points out: "To study the ancient Chinese law we must compare the codes with the books of *li;* only in this way can we trace its origin and real meaning."

11

TRANSCENDENCE IN TRADITIONAL CHINA

Huston Smith

China's regard for nature, as expressed (for example) in Sung landscape painting, is clear and well recognised. What the Chinese believed to exceed the natural world, the realm of "the ten-thousand things," is less clear. The present essay tries to explore this question systematically.

We must first distinguish between the views of the peasants and those of the intelligentsia. Peasants believed the unseen world to be peopled by innumerable spirits, both benign (*shen*) and malevolent (*kuei*), who could dwell in idols and natural objects and be used or warded off by magic and sacrifice. After Buddhism reached China the geography of the spirit world was mapped in 33 Buddhist heavens, 81 Taoist heavens, and 18 Buddhist hells. Divination, astrology, almanacs, dream interpretations, geomancy, and witchcraft all figured as ways of establishing relations with invisible powers.

We shall not linger over this popular view of the supernatural. In essence it is the Chinese version of folk religion which, where not dispelled by Enlightenment modes of thought, has been universal throughout human history. What interests us here is the way the transcendent appeared to the Chinese intelligentsia—scholars, administrators, and landed gentry.

A common answer, from Voltaire to James Legge and Hu Shih, is that transcendence scarcely figured in the outlook of the literati at

"Transcendence in Traditional China" by Huston Smith. From *Religious Studies* 2: 185–96. Reprinted by permission of the author and Cambridge University Press. Original footnotes have been deleted.

all. A representative statement asserts that "Confucius confined his attention to reality, and his views are incompatible with religious matters." Chinese intellectuals, by this view, were humanists, rationalists, and moralists. When they referred to heaven or took part in sacrifices it was from force of mechanical habit, or to provide sops for the sentiments of the masses.

Four things work to encourage this interpretation of the Chinese outlook. (1) The social accent of her outlook produced an unusual number of philosophers and schools that were purely utilitarian: The Realists, of course; but beyond them and within the Confucian stream itself such philosophers as Yen Yuan and Tai Chen in the Ch'ing Dynasty (1644–1912) and such schools as the Yung-k'ang and Yung-chia in the Sung Dynasty (960–1279). (2) Chinese positions that are *not* exclusively utilitarian tend to appear more utilitarian than they are, because the general social bent of the Chinese mind inclines it to be more explicit about social matters even when it does not really wish to limit itself to them. (3) The utilitarian interpretation of Chinese thought fits nicely with the prejudice of modern academia which, inclining toward rational humanism, is pleased (as were Voltaire and the Enlightenment Sinophiles) to find this prejudice anticipated by the sophisticated Chinese. Concomitantly the interpretation suits the propensity of modern Chinese intellectuals who are eager to justify Chinese civilization in the face of the stronger and rationalistically oriented Western world which considers mysticism and faith in supernatural powers to be symbols of waywardness and inferiority. (4) Finally, Chinese thought patterns are apt to appear utilitarian when considered "functionally" by social scientists. Social scientists study society. As a consequence their professional biases cause them to pay particular attention to, and therefore to see most distinctly, the social aspects of what they look at. When, therefore, they look at the metaphysical and religious dimensions of cultures, it is the social roots and consequences of these dimensions that leap to view. Durkheim's concept of religion, which for fifty years has dominated sociological and anthropological studies of the subject, is the classic formulation of this bias. "The idea of society," he writes, "is the soul of religion." The gods of religion are collective representations. This means most obviously that they are ideas imposed on individual minds by the group, and more significantly that "they not only come from the collective, but the things that they express are of a social nature. The reality, which mythologies have represented under so many different forms, but which is the universal and eternal objective cause of these sensations *sui generis* out of which religious experience is made, is society."

Durkheim's mistake consists in passing from the truth that religion has social consequences and reflects social patterns in its imagery to the erroneous conclusion that it must therefore have arisen and developed for social purposes. This is like reasoning that because marriages usually produce children, children must be its object. In fact, couples often marry ahead of their schedule for children, with intent to have no children at all, or (as in old age) knowing they could not reproduce if they would. It is eminently the case that in China "the religious factor plays an important role in justifying political powers, in establishing administrative authority, in maintaining peace and order, in upholding civic values, and in inspiring faith in the government and raising public morale during public crises." But it is also the case that China's "sacrificial and ritualistic activities were carried out for a sense of awe, wonder and gratitude toward an unfathomable power which can never be explained simply in socio-economic and psychological terms alone." Reviewing the role the Mandate of Heaven has played in Chinese history, a Chinese *sociologist* sees it as a device whereby "the awe and respect for the supernatural . . . put . . . the coat of morality and honour on a dynastic founder, who was basically a master manipulator of force and violence." The retort of a Chinese *humanist* is that

> what the [sociologist] has failed to see is that the person leading the rebellion is a man of his own age and beliefs and not of ours. He would not, therefore, even dare to start a rebellion had he not been assured that the Mandate of Heaven was with him. In other words, the Mandate of Heaven was not a device to achieve political ends, but something seriously believed by both the ruler and the ruled. It was religious in a . . . profound sense.

Actually the humanist overstates his case here. There doubtless were agnostics in every age who cynically played on prevailing faith to secure their worldly ambitions. But unless such cynics had been in the minority, there would have been no prevailing faith for them to play upon.

That the numinous was real for Taoism and Buddhism, no one doubts; it is in regard to Confucianism that the question arises. We read in the *Analects*:

> The Master did not talk about extraordinary things, feats of strength, disorder, and spiritual beings. (vii, 20.)
>
> While you are not able to serve men, how can you serve their spirits? . . . While you do not know life, how can you know about death? (xi, 11.)
>
> To give one's self earnestly to the duties due to men, and, while respecting spiritual beings, to keep aloof [at a distance] from them, may be called wisdom. (vi, 20.)

But as H. G. Creel pointed out in a revealing study of this question a quarter of a century ago, of the pre-Sung commentators on these and similar passages in the *Analects,* not one saw in them signs of agnosticism, while among later commentators only four suggested that they contained such signs. The Romans may have assumed that man is the highest being there is; the Chinese, Confucians included, would have sided with the Greeks who considered such a notion *atopos,* "absurd" (Aristotle). "In spite of its preoccupation with this-worldly matters, Confucianism cannot be considered a completely rationalistic system of thought." Confucius carefully kept the numinous alive, in his admonition to "respect the spiritual being," in his close attention to sacrificial ceremonies, in his watchfulness toward Heaven and its decrees. The formalised Confucianism about which we sometimes read, the Confucianism that is all exterior with no sensitivity to inwardness and the hidden mystery into which all of life's roots ultimately invisibly descend—this is fossilised Confucianism where it is Confucianism at all. The *li* which stood at the heart of Confucianism-alive was a tap-root fixed in the mystery of the Tao which, where not cut by selfishness, kept both individuals and society in living touch with Heaven's majestic will.

We labour this point because it constitutes the chief barrier to accurate assessment of the traditional Chinese outlook. No more than the masses did the Chinese intelligentsia see the world as a disenchanted causal mechanism floating on a foundation of nothingness. The principal terms by which they referred to the transcendental "more" that envelops and permeates the phenomenal world were "*T'ien* (Heaven)" and "*Tao* (Way)." The former tends to be associated with Confucianism, the latter with Taoism. The differences between these complementary strains in the Chinese persuasion are more than terminological. The Taoists were in love with nature, the Confucians with history. This meant that the Taoists tended to stress the importance of keeping human nature, "the uncarved block," undefiled, while the Confucians searched the past to discover which social patterns reflected *T'ien* most faithfully. "The essential difference is the difference between Lao-tzu's direct way to the *Tao* and Confucius' detour by way of the human order . . . Lao-tzu immerses himself in (the *Tao*), while Confucius lets himself be guided by his awe of [it] as he moves among the things of the world." But the differences are in approach and emphasis only. No more than Lao-tzu did Confucius take the community as an absolute. Both believed man and nature to be undergirded by an eternal numinous reality from which life proceeds and which inclines it toward harmony.

We can summarise the metaphysics of the Chinese literati in five points:

1. Both men and Heaven, both the phenomenal realm and the noumenal realm, are real. Underlying the visible is something of immense importance that is invisible.

2. The essential relation between the two is unity or non-duality. Life's dependability, mingling with nature's, betokens a hidden oneness in the bosom of the multiple, a total interdependence at the heart of the spheres. In this respect Chinese metaphysical thought simply instances the correlative character of Chinese thought generally. Many Chinese terms, such as "*li* (principle)," "*ming* (ordinance)," "*tao*," "*teh* (power)," and "*yang-yin*," apply to Heaven and man equally. *Tien ming*, for instance, the Heavenly Ordinance, "exists neither externally in Heaven only, nor internally in man only; it exists, rather, in the mutuality of Heaven and man; i.e., in their mutual influence and response, their mutual giving and receiving." Other terms, like "God (*ti*)," "pneuma (*ch'i*)," "grand polarity (*t'ai-chi*)," "non-polarity (*wu-chi*)," "the

Origin (*yuan*)," and "non-being (*wu*)," refer primarily to Heaven but are manifest and function in man also. Still others, such as "mind," "emotion," "desire," and "ambition," denote human qualities while connoting that these qualities have their sources in Heaven. A rhythm falls upon the visible, breaking it into day and night, summer and winter, male and female, but these divisions are caught up and ordered in a superior integration, the *Tao,* which resolves the tensions and reconciles the apparently irreconcilable. As the *Great Commentary* puts it: "Now *yin,* now *yang:* that is the *Tao.*" Heaven and earth agree. They are united in a hymn for a double choir, an antiphony on a cosmic scale. A paradigm of correlative thinking appears in those strikingly un-Semitic instances—e.g., the Chou rites for King Wen as well as for his ancestor Hou-chi—in which the Chinese joined man with Heaven and sacrificed to both in the same act.

3. In keeping with another general theme in Chinese thought, that the mutual reciprocity that pervades all things is in most instances between unequals, the relations that link man and nature are not symmetrical. Heaven is clearly the senior partner. As Confucius says: "Only Heaven is great . . . The superior man . . . stands in awe of its ordinances" (*Analects,* xvi, 8).

4. Heaven's grandeur does not, however, force it into the foreground of human thought. The Chinese perspective remains humanistic in the double sense that (*a*) man is more often than Heaven the explicit object of attention, and (*b*) when the Chinese mind does think explicitly about Heaven it usually gets at it through man by considering Heaven's relation to and import for man. Again Confucius is paradigmatic. "He who lives by *jên* has but one anxiety in his heart: not to know man" (*Analects* i, 16). In short, the Chinese were interested in man as he appears against a noumenal backdrop. He is smaller than the backdrop, but he stands out more clearly in our attention. Or if we prefer a musical analogy, the note the Chinese sounded was man, but it carried numinous overtones. The overtones were more majestic, but the note actually sounded was more distinct. "The wise man vibrates the heart of man and the universe harmonises. The one who can understand these resonances is able to understand what moves the celestial, the terrestrial, and all of creation in its multiplicity" (*I Ching,* Commentary on hexagram 31).

5. The weighting of explicit attention toward man as noted in the preceding point causes the numinous to receive in Chinese thought less sharp, objective symbolisation than it does in either India or the West. In ancient Chinese thought the numinous was personified: the character for Heaven was originally a rough sketch of a man, and in the *Odes,* the *Book of History,* and the *Tso Chuan,* Heaven loves the people and metes out rewards to the virtuous. The coming of philosophy dissolved not only this kind of anthropomorphism but all attempts to describe the numinous explicitly. Confucius never made last things his direct theme. At the approach of the ultimate he grew diffident. Seldom did he speak directly about Heaven, death, or the *Tao.* When asked about such matters he gave answers which left the questions open. We have noted the rationalist's tendency to conclude from such evasions that Confucius was a politically-minded positivist: he did not believe in the numinous but had sense enough to realise that it would be unpolitic to say so outright. For our part, having found reasons to reject this agnostic interpretation, we look to other explanations for his reticence. The principal one we have already named: his refusal to let his direct gaze be distracted from man. But beyond this, Confucius' answers to questions about the numinous left the questions open because the subject imposed such answers. Like the Buddha whose teachings were to move in and take their place beside his own, Confucius was aware at some level of the extent to which men are led to ultimate questions by inauthentic motives: idle curiosity or the wish to circumvent responsibilities at hand and thus detour the road into life. Confucius had no wish to pander to such motives. More important, he sensed intuitively what philosophers today, be they phenomenologists or analysts, are coming to see explicitly: the impossibility of discussing objectively what can never be the object of such discussion. In our time Heidegger, Jaspers, Buber and Wittgenstein have all stressed the violation that is wrought when one tries to discourse objectively about what can never, properly speaking, become an object. Ultimately it is the same perception that prompts both the *Tao Te Ching's* opening warning that "the *Tao* that can be expressed in words is not the eternal *Tao*" and Confucius' refusal to speak directly to metaphysical themes. No more than "Lao-tzu" was Confucius indifferent to the unknowable. He became chary at its mention

> because he was unwilling to deform intimation into pseudo-knowledge and lose it in words. "For him the Encompassing is a background, not a theme to work with; it is the limit and foundation to be considered with awe, not the immediate task." His certainty was rooted in the Encompassing, but it enjoined him to turn to mankind in the actual world. So we discern the presence of last things in his outlook only indirectly, "in his pious observance of customs and in maxims which, without explicitly saying much, suggest a way in critical situations." His direct concern was for beauty, harmony, integrity, and happiness in the world, but all these were grounded "in something that is not made meaningless by failure and death."

What Karl Jaspers says of Confucius in these last three quotations can be said of the Chinese intellectual position generally. The spiritual "upholds all, is imminent to all, and nothing can be separated from it" (*Doctrine of the Mean,* xiv). But it is a zone which "one contemplates without seeing, listens to without hearing" (*ibid.*). Like the cosmos itself which both manifests the *Tao* and conceals it, sages can allude to the numinous but are quickly brought to silence. "When man has examined the universe closely—the perfect alternation of days and nights, of heat and cold, their constriction as they go, their unbending as they come [again]—he reaches a point beyond which he cannot go" (paraphrased from the *I Ching,* Great Appendix, chapter v, by Confucius or his school). To understand the depths of *Tao* or the decrees of Heaven is impossible for man. "The *Tao!* How deep and unfathomable!" (*Tao Teh Ching,* Giles translation). "Heaven is what it is" (*Doctrine of the Mean,* xxvii).

So the literati alluded to Heaven more than they defined it, and they sensed it more than they alluded to it. At the same time they were shrewd enough to realise that they could not eschew symbolisation entirely or deference would turn to forgetfulness. So they sacrificed. When the Emperor offered the annual sacrifices to Heaven and magistrates gathered villagers around mounds to sacrifice to earth, peasants may have visualised gods being fed and buttered up generally to ensure their continuing benefactions. Most scholars would have had no such anthropomorphic imaginings, but they would not for this reason have deemed the sacrifices less important nor valued them solely for their effects on the masses. For gentry no less than peasants, "sacrificial and ritualistic activities were carried out for a sense of awe, wonder, and gratitude toward an unfathomable power which [could] never be explained simply in socio-economic and psychological terms." Sacrifices represented the community's collective recognition that it was not autonomous, that it was enveloped by a "more" that nurtured it as long as its divine imperatives were honoured. They constituted the Chinese way of expressing the feeling "this nation, under God."

To summarise: For the literati the noumenal was (1) real, (2) organically related to the phenomenal, (3) more majestic than the phenomenal while being (4) less in focus or rewarding for direct attention and (5) better intimated than explicitly described, better sensed than thought. What the sense provided above all else was the awareness of being related. According to a contemporary psychiatrist, this awareness is man's fundamental want. "A longing for knowing that one has roots, that one's existence reflects the order and trustworthiness and utter 'sanity' of the universe itself . . . a longing for some absolute awareness of relatedness [is] man's deepest need." China's concentric vision, the vision of society set like a stone in nature and nature set similarly in the deep repose of eternity, filled this need. If everything is tied together in an organic system of interdependent parts, man's life shades into eternity. The concept inspired a medley of profound religious institutions. One sensed the blessings of Heaven and Earth as they flowed into the society which sustained one's life. Or if taste tended toward monism, one sensed the soul of man as identical with the soul of Heaven and Earth and all things. Security was assured, for society was no holding operation, pieced together against chaos by some precarious social contract. It was man's natural condition, the condition to which cosmic sources naturally inclined man if he did not wilfully and selfishly divert them. But security was not the vision's only yield. Relatedness gave life meaning as well. An important reason for existential despondency in the contemporary West is the existentialists' conclusions that man's values are free-floating, that they have no grounding or sanction beyond his own private regard. The Chinese saw things otherwise. The values that rightly order society imbue everything. They are rooted in being itself. "The Heavenly *ming* (Ordinance) . . . and . . . 'what one's heart feels peace in' . . . are two aspects of one thing." When Confucius extolled the legendary founders of Chinese civilisation it was no idiosyncratic inventiveness that he praised. He revered them because, having perceived the eternal archetypes of heaven, they ordered their lives by them to the point where they became transparent through them. "Only heaven is great; only Yao was equal to it."

These psychological benefits which the Chinese derived from the transcendent were important, but equally important was the way it re-enforced the dutiful, social conduct they prized so dearly.

First, it provided grounds for their conviction that the social norms (*li*) which individuals should strive to exemplify in their conduct toward one another were not arbitrary. Had the Chinese suspected that these norms were no more than conventions or, worse, had been perpetrated by a segment of society to shore up its privileged position, they could have regarded them more lightly. As it was, they saw them as sanctioned by the cosmos: they were natural law. "The 'rules' . . . have their origin in Heaven and Earth, i.e., in 'the central harmony between Heaven and Earth.' " When society is ordered as it should be, when men behave human-heartedly toward one another, when rulers govern wisely and sacrifices are observed in spirit as well as form, then society, nature and cosmos combine to function like a beautifully synchronised machine. But deviate from the heaven-appointed pattern and everything will go wrong. Wars and pillage will abound. Even nature will be thrown off its track and erupt in plague and rampage.

It is in this connection that we have our best chance of understanding Confucius' "reversed time orientation," for it was in the human record that Confucius thought men have the best chance of perceiving what the heavenly sanctioned values are. If Confucius has been mistaken for a rationalist, he has been mistaken oftener for a conservative. The mistake is understandable for he did characterise himself as "a transmitter and not a maker, believing in and loving the ancients." But we must be careful, in reading this sentence, making sure in particular that we balance it with his seemingly opposite assertion that "a man born in our days who returns to the ways of antiquity is a fool and brings misfortune upon himself." As no uncomplicated conservative could have said that, we do better to read Confucius' attitude as historical rather than conservative in any mechanical sense. He loved the past, but not for itself so much as for the fact that it is there that we see the woof of man's doings laid out on the warp of eternity. This makes it the place where normative values become most clearly evident, ideally through exemplification, but if not, then through their conspicuous absence. To embody these values in the present calls not for blindly reduplicating the past but for translating what was good within it into contemporary idiom. Repetition of the eternally valid, this rather than imitation of empirical history was his object. Only on this interpretation could Karl Jaspers say of him: "Here for the first time in history a great philosopher shows how the new, merging with the tradition flowing from the source of eternal truth, becomes the substance of our existence."

If the Confucians loved history, the Taoists loved nature. Here we come upon a second way in which the Chinese sense of the transcendent supported appropriate social conduct; namely, by imbuing her people with the sense that human nature inclines toward appropriate conduct in a kind of natural tropism. Instead of scanning the past to see which attitudes and acts go well and which do not, the Taoists advocated centring down to "the uncarved block," man's original unspoiled, Tao-endowed nature, believing that if we could unburden ourselves of society's warping effects we would all behave very well. Though the Taoists were unique in staking everything on this "return to the source," the notion that man is naturally inclined toward virtue is widespread in Chinese thought. Very early the *Odes* tell us that "Heaven gives birth to the people. If there is a thing there is a rule for it; therefore the nature of the people will naturally incline to virtue." Confucius continued the refrain—"True goodness springs from man's own heart . . . Is virtue so far away?"—while Mencius went "much further than Confucius in his insistence upon the goodness of human nature . . . teaching . . . that since human nature is endowed by heaven, it must be good." "Man's natural tendency toward goodness is like the water's tendency to find the lower level," he wrote. The ancient sage kings were simply men who fully developed their innate goodness.

With the passing of the centuries the debate over whether man is innately good was to deteriorate into pedantic bickering and trivial scholasticism. But in the formative stages of Chinese thought the question was vital. For our image of ourselves affects our conduct: we do not always behave like the kind of person we think we are, but we tend to do so. To believe that one's fundamental nature participates in the transcendent source of all goodness, call it Tao or T'ien, is to be disposed to some extent to act accordingly.

Though man is naturally inclined toward virtue, this inclination is at birth, as Mencius says, only a tender shoot which must be nurtured and developed. This brings us to a third way in which the transcendent re-enforced appropriate social conduct: it rewarded virtue's cultivation. In ancient times this reward meant worldly prosperity. Thus we read in the *Book of Odes* that Heaven cherished the illustrious virtue of King Wen, and so the Heavenly Ordinance (*ming*), which would ensure a successful reign, came upon him. With the coming of sophistication, Heaven's reward came to be conceived more inwardly, moving toward a Chinese version of virtue as its own reward. It continued to be assumed that the Heavenly Ordinance would descend on the man who cultivated his virtue, though it might be clearer at this stage to say that the virtuous man's life would become aligned with the *ming;* but the *ming* for the individual (the *ming* for the ruler was a different matter) no longer implied worldly success. "It does not necessarily follow that upon the man who 'receives the Heavenly *ming*' God will definitely bestow wealth and high rank, and make him the actual king . . . [Being] unlimited . . . the . . . Tao may be realised equally in the outward success and the outward failure of men." This drift of thought led directly to Chuang Tzu's concept of the man of virtue as one who is in complete harmony with whatever transpires. Through unswerving loyalty and filial piety man becomes indifferent to both pleasure and grief. The man who preserves his inner harmony and spiritual glory will be so attuned to the operation of *ming* amidst variable circumstances that he will be in accord with whatever happens. From this premise Chuang Tzu proceeds to his ideas of "enjoying one's heart in accordance with things as they are" and "non-differentiation of things leading to a state of untroubled ease." The man whose heart has come to rest in *ming* is indifferent to circumstances in pursuing his duty, even to death. "Death and life are great considerations, but they could work no change in him. Though Heaven and Earth were to be overturned and fall, they would occasion him no loss." "I and

Heaven and Earth are born together, and I and all things in the universe are in a state of unity." Amidst these changing concepts of the character of reward, the constant element was the notion that things in their widest and most ultimate context, are set up in such a way that, whether visibly or invisibly, grossly or subtly, outwardly or inwardly, virtue brings satisfaction.

Fourth, the transcendent supported social conduct by encouraging its development beyond any given stage that it actually reached. This comes out in the idea that "the Heavenly *ming* is not unchangeable" (*Book of Odes* and *Book of History*). Were it unchangeable, a man who developed a modicum of virtue could rest on his oars, content with the Heavenly blessing that came with the virtue he had acquired. In point of fact, however, " 'acceptance of Heavenly *ming*', in its true meaning, is . . . the starting point of something to be done, rather than a terminal point of something already accomplished. . . . Once one has received *ming* he must further cultivate his virtue." The reason he must do so can be stated both positively—"The more fully men cultivate their virtue, the more fully will heaven confer its mandate on them"—and negatively: those who fail to keep cultivating their virtue will find Heaven's blessing withdrawn.

Such statements obviously point to a relationship in which "there is mutual influence and response between Heaven and men." In his discussion of "correlative thinking" and "resonance" in the second volume of *Science and Civilization in China,* Joseph Needham describes this relationship with great penetration. Here, with limited space, we try to reach its essential point through cybernetics:

> Cybernetics is not just a technological revolution; it is a revolution in our way of thinking. . . .
>
> Western man has traditionally thought . . . in terms of cause and effect going in one direction. That is, if A causes B, B cannot cause A. The reason for this assumption is that event order has been confused with logical order; Western man has assumed that because "circular argument" is prohibited in logic, there cannot be circular causal relationships in natural or social events.
>
> But not everyone has thought this way . . . Peoples in pre-communist China . . . have seen the universe as a mutual process of . . . influences in harmony and occasionally disturbed harmony

> —in complementary balance rather than in vertical opposition . . .
> In a sense they have been living cybernetically . . . Cybernetics [in one of its aspects] is concerned with the growth, development, and the rise of complex structures resulting from *mutual* interactions between components which do not fall into a causal hierarchy.[1]

The relation between the Heavenly *ming* and human effort constituted an important instance of such mutual interaction. The more man exerted himself in the cultivation of his virtue the more the Heavenly mandate blessed his efforts and strengthened their continuance. The more his efforts slackened, the further the mandate receded and the more difficult it became for him to renew his moral exertion.

Finally, in all of the four ways we have enumerated, the transcendent encouraged political as well as private morality. The Emperor's position was not simply that of the man who had risen to the top of violence's heap. He ruled with the Mandate of Heaven for the benefit of the world under Heaven. As this Mandate is unceasing—"Heaven constantly loves the people and therefore looks on all parts of the world to find a dwelling place for its mandate, which it confers unceasingly"—if one Emperor's regime ceased to furnish the Mandate a fitting abode, Heaven would be forced to spot and back to victory a new Emperor whose regime would renew the hospitality.

1.[Magoroh Maruyama, "Cybernetics," *NEA Journal* (December, 1964), pp. 51–52. By the same author, "The Second Cybernetics," *American Scientist,* 51 in nos. 2 and 3 (1963).]

12

THE EVOLUTION OF THE FUNDAMENTAL CONCEPT IN CONFUCIANISM

Wing-tsit Chan

The concept of *jên* (pronounced *ren*) is one of the most important in Chinese thought. The very fact that *"jên"* has been translated into many English terms—benevolence, love, altruism, kindness, charity, compassion, magnanimity, perfect virtue, goodness, true manhood, manhood at its best, human-heartedness, humaneness, humanity, "hominity," man-to-manness—shows that it is an exceedingly complicated concept. Not only is it the backbone of Confucianism, but it also ranks very high in the Buddhist and Taoist scales of value. In Buddhism, the word *"jên"* has long been used as an honorific for the Buddha, a worthy person, a temple, or a pagoda. It is true that in ancient Taoist classics *jên* is severely denounced as hypocrisy, but eventually the leading philosopher of religious Taoism, Ko Hung (253–333?) incorporated it into the Taoist ethical system as a cardinal virtue.

But *jên* is essentially a Confucian concept, and it was Confucius (551–479) who made it really significant. . . . Chinese scholars agree that *jên* in the ancient Classics connotes a particular virtue, namely, kindness of a ruler to his people.

In Confucius, however, all of this is radically changed. In the first place, Confucius made *jên* the central theme of his conversations. In

From "The Evolution of the Confucian Concept *Jên*" by Wing-tsit Chan, *Philosophy East and West* 4 (1954–55): 295–319. Excerpted and reprinted by permission of the University of Hawaii Press. Footnotes have been deleted.

the *Analects,* 58 of the 499 chapters are devoted to the discussion of *jên,* and the word appears 105 times. No other subject, not even filial piety, engaged so much of the attention of the Master and his disciples. . . .

Furthermore, instead of perpetuating the ancient understanding of *jên* as a particular virtue, he transformed it into what Legge very appropriately translated as "perfect virtue" and Waley as "Goodness." To be sure, in a few cases *jên* is still used by Confucius as a particular virtue. For example, in *Analects* IV. 2; VI. 21; IX. 28 (repeated in XIV. 30); XV. 32; and XVII. 8, *jên* is contrasted with knowledge, wisdom, courage, or propriety. In this narrow sense, *jên* is best translated as "benevolence," as Legge has done. In all other cases, however, *jên* connotes the general meaning of moral life at its best. It includes filial piety (XVII. 21), wisdom (V. 18), propriety (XII. 1), courage (XIV. 5), and loyalty to government (V. 18; XVIII. 1); it requires the practice of "earnestness, liberality, truthfulness, diligence, and generosity" (XVII. 6); it is more than the "refraining from love of superiority, boasting, resentment, and covetousness" (XIV. 2); and it underlies ceremonies and music (III. 3). It consists in "mastering oneself and returning to propriety" (XII. 1). One who is "strong, resolute, simple, and slow in speech is near to" but still falls short of *jên* (XIII. 27). A man of *jên* is respectful in private life, earnest in handling affairs, and loyal in his association with people" (XIII. 19), "serves the most worthy among the great officers and makes friends of the most virtuous among scholars" (XV. 9), and is cautious and slow in speech (XII. 3). On the other hand, "a man with clever words and an ingratiating appearance seldom possesses *jên*" (I. 3). One who "keeps his jewel in his bosom and leaves his country to confusion" cannot be called a man of *jên* (XVII. 1). "Those without *jên* cannot abide long either in a condition of poverty and hardship or in a condition of enjoyment" (IV. 2). In short, *jên* precludes all evil and underlies as well as embraces all possible virtues, so much so that "if you set your mind on *jên,* you will be free from evil" (IV. 4). In other words, a man of *jên* is a perfect man. "He alone knows how to love others and to hate others" (IV. 3). He seeks *jên* so eagerly that "when it comes to *jên,* he will compete even with his teacher" (XV. 35). He cherishes *jên* so highly that he "will never seek to live at the expense of *jên* and would rather sacrifice his life in order to realize it" (XV. 8). When he has fully realized *jên,* he becomes a sage (VI. 28; VII. 33). . . .

As the general virtue, *jên* is no longer a special moral characteristic of rulers but a quality applicable to all human beings. This is another important contribution Confucius made to the evolution of the concept of *jên.* It is amazing that, although many of Confucius' conversations with his disciples concern government, yet in no instance did he use the word *jên* as a special quality of rulers. On the contrary, it denotes a quality of man as such. Whenever he discussed *jên,* he referred to it in relation to man as man. There are only a few sayings in which *jên* specifically concerns rulers (V. 7; VI. 28; XII. 20; XVII. 6), and in none of these does *jên* carry the idea of kindness from a superior. Instead, the emphasis is that *jên* is a virtue particularly difficult for a ruler to achieve. All this amounts to an ethical revolution, for a moral quality that formerly belonged to aristocrats now belongs to all men.

But what is this general virtue in concrete terms? Confucius offered neither a precise definition nor a comprehensive description. However, when a pupil asked him about *jên,* he replied, "It is to love man" (XII. 22). We have here the key word to the Confucian doctrine, namely *"ai"* love. It is on the basis of this meaning, no doubt, that the standard Chinese dictionary, the *Shuo-wên* (A.D. 100), defines *jên* as "affection" (*ch'in*). It is also on this basis that ancient Chinese philosophers, whether Confucian, Taoist, Moist, or Legalist, and practically all Han Confucianists have equated *jên* with love.

As to the extent of this love, two questions arise. The first is whether it can be called the Golden Rule. It is often contended in the West that the Confucian doctrine of love is negative because it taught "Do not do to others what you do not want others to do to you" (XII. 2; XV. 23; the *Doctrine of the Mean,* 13). But followers of Confucius have never understood it as negative. Mencius (371–289?), who should have understood Confucius, quoting the Confucian phrase "Not to do to others," included both the negative and positive aspects in his elaboration. He said, "There is a way to win their [the people's] hearts. It is to give them and keep for them what is liked and not to do to them what is not liked." Commentators on the *Analects* in the last eighteen centuries have never understood the

Golden Rule to be negative. In his *Lun-yü chêng-i* ("Correct Meanings of the *Analects*"), for example, Liu Pao-nan (1791–1855) made this comment: "Do not do to others what you do not want others to do to you. Then by necessity we must do to others what we want them to do to us."

Thus we see that the Golden Rule of Confucius has both a negative and a positive aspect. This positive aspect is by no means merely an implication but a clear and unmistakable expression of Confucius. "There are four things in the moral life of a man," he said,

> no one of which I have been able to carry out in my life. To serve my father as I would expect my son to serve me: that I have not been able to do. To serve my sovereign as I would expect a minister under me to serve me. . . . To act toward my elder brother as I would expect my younger brother to act toward me. . . . To be the first to behave toward friends as I would expect them to behave toward me. . . . (the *Doctrine of the Mean,* 13).

Or, to quote the *Analects,* "The man of *jên,* wishing to establish his own character, also seeks to establish the character of others. Wishing to succeed, he also seeks to help others succeed. To be able to judge of others by what is near in ourselves, this may be the method of achieving *jên*" (VI. 28). . . .

It is only in the light of the stress on particularity that we can understand certain apparent contradictions in Confucian sayings. *Jên* is sometimes regarded as very easy (IV. 6; VI. 28; VII. 29) but sometimes very difficult to achieve (XIV. 2). In some cases, the sacrifice of one's life is considered *jên* (VI. 14; XV, 8); in others, not sacrificing one's life is so considered (XIV. 17–18). Not to remonstrate one's superior is *jên,* but to remonstrate even unto death is also *jên* (XVIII. 1). To one pupil *jên* is cultivation of the inner life, but to another its value consists in proper external conduct (XII. 1-2).

However, such apparent contradictions are not difficult to understand if one remembers that Confucius was not interested in abstract concepts. He was not concerned with the reality or nature of *jên*; he was interested primarily in its application. Since individuals and circumstances differ, its exemplification naturally takes different or even opposite forms. Thus, to six different pupils who asked about *jên* he gave six different answers, each according to the pupil's temperament, capability, or environment (XII. 1, 2, 3, 22; XV. 9; XVII. 6). Generally speaking, however, there can be no doubt that *jên* is love for all. . . .

[Nevertheless,] in the eyes of Confucianists, universal love of the Moist type was both unnatural and impracticable. These two points have been emphasized by many Confucianists, but most strongly by Wang Yang-ming (Wang Shou-jên, 1472–1529). Love should start with filial piety toward parents, he said, just as a tree should start with a sprout. This, he contended, is where Confucianism is superior to Moism, for in the universal love of Moism there is no central point for the seed to sprout. This argument is no sheer analogy, but is based on the law of nature. For anything to grow, it must have a starting point, and, given the ideal conditions, the growth will extend to the limit. Therefore, he said, "Show affection to my parents, then to other people's parents, and then to the parents of all people in the world. Only then does my *jên* form one body with all parents."

But it is not only natural that love should start with one's parents; it is also a matter of practical necessity. He said,

> We love both our nearest relatives and strangers. Nevertheless, when there is only little food, so that with it we will survive and without it we will perish, and we cannot save both relatives and strangers, under such circumstances we will have to save our nearest relatives. . . . What the *Great Learning* calls relative importance is, in our native knowledge, a natural order of procedure.

But the support of the doctrine of love with distinctions is not confined to these practical considerations. There is also a metaphysical basis, which was provided by Chang Tsai (Chang Hêng-ch'ü, 1020–1077). This is not to say that Chang was the first to treat the subject of *jên* metaphysically. In a sense, that point was reached as early as the *Doctrine of the Mean* and the *Book of Mencius*. In the *Doctrine of the Mean,* 20 it is declared that "*Jên* (love) is *jên* (man)." This is more than a pun or an echo of the ancient usage of *jên* (man) for *jên* (love). Rather, for the first time in history, it carries the concept to a metaphysical level, from which Confucius kept himself at a safe distance. By identifying *jên* with human nature, however, the *Doctrine of the Mean* opens a new chapter in the evolution of the *jên* doctrine. When *jên* is viewed thus, Western translations such as "humanity," "humaneness," "true manhood" (Lin Yutang), "manhood at its best" (Ware), and "hominity" (Boodberg) are particularly appropriate.

Mencius went a step further, not only by strengthening the metaphysical trend with the repetition of the sentence "*Jên* is *jên*" (VIIB. 16), but also by providing a psychological explanation, saying, "*Jên* is man's mind" (VIA. 11). He says further, "The sense of commiseration is the beginning of *jên*" (IIA. 6), by which he means that "all men have a mind that cannot bear [to see the suffering of] others" (IIA. 6; VIIB. 31). He also said, "The sense of commiseration is *jên*" (VIA. 6). In this sense of *jên* as the human mind or heart, it is most correctly rendered by Lucius Porter as "human-heartedness."

The metaphysical trend, having started in the *Doctrine of the Mean* and Mencius, was reinforced by the theory that *jên* is man's nature, while love is his feeling. The *Comprehensive Discussions in the White Tiger Hall* (*Po-hu t'ung*) of the first century states, "In man's nature there is *jên*." Han Yü made the distinction even clearer, saying, "What constitutes man's nature consists of five [virtues]: namely, *jên,* propriety, good faith, righteousness, and wisdom. And man's feelings consist of these seven, namely, joy, anger, sorrow, fear, love, hate, and desire." Because of such distinction, the Neo-Confucian philosopher Ch'êng I (Ch'êng I-ch'uan, 1033–1107) refused to regard *jên* and love as synonymous. He said, "Since Mencius said that the sense of commiseration is *jên,* scholars have considered love as *jên*. But love is man's feeling, whereas *jên* is man's nature. . . . The sense of commiseration is only the beginning of *jên*. . . . It is incorrect to equate universal love with *jên*." To him, as to other Neo-Confucianists, *jên* is a reality, while love is a function. In making such a distinction, these philosophers made two contributions at the same time, namely, treating *jên* as a metaphysical reality and distinguishing it from love.

However, the credit for providing a metaphysical explanation for the doctrine of love with distinctions goes to Chang Tsai. In his famous *Western Inscription,* he declares, "Heaven is my father and

Earth is my mother, and such a small creature as I find an intimate place in their midst. . . . All people are my brothers and sisters, and all things are my companions." Although the inscription is very short, it exercised tremendous influence on the thinking of Chinese philosophers at his time and has ever since. Its primary purpose, as Yang Kuei-shan (1053–1135) pointed out, was to urge the student to seek *jên*. Here is an important development, namely, that *jên* not only means the love of all people but the love of all things as well. In other words, love is truly universalized.

Is this universalization of *jên* an extension of the Moist universal love? From the fact that Chang employed the term *"chien-ai,"* universal or mutual love, a term which the Moists repeatedly used but which no other Confucianist had ever employed, one is tempted to surmise that philosopher Chang was under Moist influence. Such, however, is not the case. The term *"chien-ai"* was not confined to Moist writing. It was also used by non-Moists, Yang Hsiung (53 B.C.–A.D. 18), the Confucian-Taoist, for example. Furthermore, the chapter in which the term occurs in Chang's work, as Chu Hsi noted in his commentary, is devoted particularly to a discussion of Chang's basic idea that "the Principle (*li*) is differentiated into distinctions and gradations." This refers to the epoch-making theory formulated by Chang, namely, the theory of *li-i fên-shu,* that is, the Principle is one but its function is differentiated into the many. As Chang Tsai said, "The Great Vacuity is the essence of the Material Force. . . . It is in reality one. When the active and passive Material Forces are disintegrated, they become the many." This is not an undifferentiated continuum, but a unity full of clear distinctions. "The Great Harmony is called the Way (*Tao,* Moral Law)," he said. "It embraces the nature which underlies all counter processes of floating and sinking, rising and falling, and motion and rest. It is the origin of the process of fusion and intermingling, of overcoming and being overcome, and of expansion and contradiction." While he asserts that "nothing stands isolated," he at the same time maintains that "no two of the products of creation are alike." This doctrine that "the Principle is one but its function is differentiated into the many" has become a keynote in the entire course of Confucianism during the last eight hundred years.

When this doctrine is applied to *jên,* the harmony of universal love and love with distinctions is clear. In his commentary on the *Western Inscription,* Chu Hsi (1130–1200) had this to say:

> There is nothing in the entire realm of creatures that does not regard Heaven as the father and Earth as the mother. This means that the Principle is one. . . . Each regards his parents as his own parents and his son as his own son. This being the case, how can the Principle not be differentiated into the many? . . . When the intense affection for parents is extended to broaden the impartiality that knows no ego, and when sincerity in serving one's parents leads to the understanding of the way to serve Heaven, then everywhere there is the operation that "the Principle is one but its function is differentiated into the many."

This is the metaphysical basis for the Confucian doctrine of love with distinctions, which Mencius so vigorously defended. As Yang Kuei-shan observed, "As we know, the Principle is one, and that is why there is love. The functions are many, and that is why there is righteousness. . . . Since functions are different, the applications [of love] cannot be without distinctions."

Because Chang and later Neo-Confucianists all maintained that *jên,* like existence in general, is a synthesis of universality and particularity, it is hard to agree with F.S.C. Northrop, who considers *jên* to be "the basic *tao* of Taoism," describes *jên* as "indeterminate," repeatedly speaks of *jên* together with *Tao, Nirvāna,* and *Brahman,* and states,

> It appears that *jên* in Confucianism, Tao in Taoism, Nirvāna in Buddhism, and Brahman or Ātman or Chit in Hinduism and Jainism are all to be identified with the immediately apprehended aesthetic component in the nature of things, and with this in its all-embracing indeterminateness, after all sensed distinctions are abstracted.

He later uses the phrase, "the source of *jên*" as equivalent to *Brahman, Ātman, Nirvāna,* and *Tao.* Whatever he may have in mind, he ignores the glaring fact that the Confucian *jên,* which includes particulars and determinateness, is different from *Nirvāna, Tao, Brahman,* etc., where differences completely disappear.

The amazing thing about Chang Tsai's concept of *jên* is that, while love, because of the principle of the many, cannot be without distinctions, at the same time, by virtue of the principle of the one, love is extended to encompass the entire universe. With this he started a whole current of thought that was to characterize Neo-Confucianism thereafter.

There is no doubt that this idea reflects Buddhist influence, for hitherto Confucian love had been confined largely to the mundane world, whereas the object of moral consciousness in Buddhism is the entire universe. Yang Kuei-shan thinks that Chang Tsai's doctrine comes from Mencius' saying, "The superior man is affectionate to his parents and is *jên* toward all people. He is *jên* toward all people and loves (*ai*) all things." But "things" in the quotation refers only to living beings, whereas Chang extends *jên* to cover the whole realm of existence. The upshot of this extension is the all-important doctrine of "forming one body with the universe."

This doctrine received strong impetus in the Ch'êng brothers (Ch'êng Hao, also called Ch'êng Ming-tao, 1032–1085, and his younger brother, Ch'êng I). In his celebrated treatise on *jên,* the *Shih-jên p'ien* ("On Understanding the Nature of *Jên*"), which has been a *vade mecum* of many a Chinese scholar, Ch'êng Hao begins, "The student must first of all understand the nature of *jên*. The man of *jên* forms one body with all things comprehensively." Elsewhere he says, "The man of *jên* regards the universe and all things as one body." Ch'êng I said, "The man of *jên* regards Heaven and Earth and all things as one body." Their utterances have become so familiar that they, rather than Chang Tsai, have come to be regarded as the originators of the doctrine.

From the time of Chang Tsai, all Neo-Confucianists have elaborated or at least repeated the idea. Among them, Wang Yang-ming has been generally recognized as the strongest champion of the doctrine. He said,

> The great man regards Heaven and Earth and the myriad things as one body. He regards the world as one family and the country as one person. As for those who make a cleavage between objects and distinguish between the self and others, they are small men. That the great man can regard Heaven, Earth, and the myriad things as one body is not because he deliberately wants to do so, but it is natural

> with the loving nature of his mind that he forms a unity with Heaven, Earth, and the myriad things.

In our own day this doctrine is advocated both by Fung Yu-lan (1895—), who before his submission to Communism was considered the leader of the Rationalistic wing of twentieth-century Neo-Confucianism, and by Hsiung Shih-li (1885–1968), leader of twentieth-century Neo-Confucian Idealism.

It is to be noted that the extension of *jên* to cover the entire universe is in no sense a metaphysical flight or escape from the human world. The Confucian unity with the universe is quite different from Taoist unity with the universe, especially in Chuang Tzŭ. Taoist unity is strictly individualistic and completely quietistic. It is, on the one hand, a personal affair and, on the other, a state of mind, whereas Confucian *jên,* whether applied to human beings or to things, is essentially social and active. These two qualities—sociality and activity—are its outstanding characteristics, and they can be traced back to Confucius. For the sage and his followers, *jên* finds its real meaning only in practical application. *Jên* is first and foremost an activity, not a state of mind. An overwhelming portion of Confucian aphorisms on *jên* deal with what to *do* and how to *act.* As will be shown later, Confucianists have repeatedly rejected the theory that *jên* is only or predominantly a state of mind. They have insisted that *jên* is not a virtue to be contemplated on but a principle to be carried out. In view of this, it is difficult to accept Waley's assertion that "*jên* is a mystic entity not merely analogous to but in certain sayings practically identical with the Tao of the Quietists." Only one Confucian saying indicates that "the man of *jên* is quiet" (VI. 21). In contrast to this, the man of *jên,* "after having performed his moral duties, employs his time and energy in cultural studies" (I. 6); in selecting a residence, he fixes on one where *jên* prevails (IV. 1); he "applies his strength to *jên*" (IV. 6); and he confers benefits upon and assists all (VI. 28). If, on the strength of VII. 29 ("Is *jên* remote? As soon as I want, it is right by me"), IV. 5 ("A superior man does not, even for the space of a single meal, violate *jên*"), or VI. 5 ("For as long as three months Hui's mind does not violate *jên*"), one is to conclude that *jên* is mystical, one would be going too far indeed, for neither eagerness nor attentiveness is the monopoly of a *yogin*. . . .

The other characteristic of *jên,* its sociality, has far-reaching significance and is directly opposed to an isolated individual state of being. While Confucius was an arch champion of individual perfection, he did not think of an individual as isolated from his fellow beings. In the Confucian scheme of things, not only does an individual necessarily exist in society, but his perfection cannot be achieved except within society. There are few Confucian aphorisms which can be construed as referring to the individual in isolation. One might turn to IV. 2 ("The man of *jên* is naturally at home with *jên*"); VII. 6 ("Set your mind on the Way, hold fast to virtue, follow the principle of *jên,* and seek enjoyment in the arts"); and IX. 28 ("The man of *jên* has no worry"—repeated in XIV. 30), as well as some sayings already quoted, notably IV. 4, 5; VI. 5, 21; VII. 29; and his pupil's saying in XIX. 6. But in the first place there is nothing in any of these utterances to prevent *jên* from being applied to man in society. In the second place, all other sayings on the subject concern one's relation with other men. . . . Thus *jên* becomes meaningless unless it is involved in actual human relationships. This is the reason Chêng Hsüan (127–200) defined it as "people living together" (*jên-hsiang-ou*).

Since the nature of *jên* can be fully realized only in society, any attempt to conceive of it as a state of mind would be Buddhistic and Taoistic and utterly un-Confucian. For this reason, Chou Tun-i's substitute of impartiality (*kung*) for *jên* and Hsieh Liang-tso's theory of *jên* as consciousness were both rejected by their fellow Neo-Confucianists. Chou Tun-i (Chou Lien-hsi, 1017–73), who may be considered the founder of the Neo-Confucian movement, said, "The Way of the sage is nothing other than absolute impartiality." Again, he said, "Whoever is impartial toward himself will be impartial toward others. There has never been a person who is partial toward himself and yet can be impartial toward others." *Jên* as the cardinal virtue is now replaced by impartiality. To Chou Tun-i, impartiality is not only an ethical quality, that of equal consideration for the self and others. It also has a metaphysical overtone, for it means the non-distinction of the internal and the external, and of the refined and the gross. The Buddhist influence here is obvious. Chou went even further and said that to be impartial one must be "without desire." This is clearly quietistic, devoid of the dynamic and active qualities of Confucian love. Further, it is an individual state of mind, devoid of actual social relations. Such a Buddhistic virtue was utterly intolerable to the Confucianists. It had to be either repudiated or reconstructed. The latter course was chosen and was pursued by Ch'êng I, who said,

> Essentially speaking, the way of *jên* may be expressed in one word, namely, impartiality. However, impartiality is but the principle of *jên;* it should not be equated with *jên* itself. When man puts impartiality into practice, that is *jên*. Because of impartiality, one can accommodate both others and himself. Therefore, a man of *jên* is a man of both altruism and love. Altruism is the application of *jên*, while love is its function.

The importance of the passage is not only that it distinguishes impartiality and *jên* by saying that "impartiality is the principle of *jên*" but also that it insists that impartiality must be practiced or embodied in action (*t'i-chih*). Only when that is done does it become *jên*. The point of practice makes the whole difference between transcendental and quietistic Buddhism, on the one hand, and active and humanistic Confucianism, on the other. A real virtue must be *demonstrated.* Fung Yu-lan is wrong in taking *t'i-chih* to mean *t'i-tieh,* that is, sympathetic feeling toward others' feelings. Such an interpretation makes it no less individualistic and quietistic and therefore Buddhistic. Ch'êng I explicitly talked about the "application of *jên*" and the "function of *jên*." The weight is on actual demonstration in society. Chu Hsi commented on the above passage, "All the work to be done lies in the word 'man.' "

Similar objections were raised against Hsieh Liang-tso's description of *jên* as consciousness. Hsieh (1050–1103) says:

> What is *jên?* That which is alive is *jên* and that which is dead is not *jên*. We call paralysis of the body and the unconsciousness of feeling the absence of *jên*. . . . Those Buddhists who understand this claim that they have thus discovered their true nature and there is nothing more to do. Hence, they finally result in falsehood and

absurdities. Students of the Confucian school, on the other hand, having observed such things, will make a special effort.

Hsieh was explicitly anti-Buddhist, and in his insistence on making an effort he was a true Confucianist. But he also pronounced a new theory in these words: "When there is the consciousness of pain in case of illness, we call it *jên*." In other words, Hsieh unmistakably identified *jên* with consciousness, which is a new departure in Confucianism. Other Neo-Confucianists had reduced *jên* to a state of mind, but none had regarded *jên* as consciousness itself. In this respect, he spoke like a Buddhist. As a matter of fact, he actually used the Buddhist term *chiao,* consciousness, and definitely identified it with *jên*. "*Jên* is the awareness of pain [in case of illness]. The Confucianists call it *jên,* while the Buddhists call it consciousness." Such a Buddhist doctrine could hardly be attractive to Neo-Confucianists. In criticism of it, Ch'êng I said, "One who is not *jên* is not conscious of anything. But it is incorrect to consider consciousness as *jên*." Later Chu Hsi frankly stated, "In over-emphasizing the concept of consciousness, Hsieh Liang-tso seems to be expounding the doctrines of the Buddhist Meditation School."

When Hsieh used the analogy of paralysis, he was paraphrasing Ch'êng Hao, who was the first to use it and make it famous. This is what Ch'êng said:

> Books on medicine describe paralysis of the four limbs as absence of *jên*. This is an excellent description. . . . If things are not parts of the self, naturally they have nothing to do with it. As in the case of paralysis of the four limbs, the vital force no longer penetrates them, and therefore they are no longer parts of myself. Therefore, to be charitable and to assist all things is the function of the sage. . . . Therefore, Confucius merely said that the man of *jên,* "wishing to establish his own character, also seeks to establish the character of others, and, wishing to succeed, also seeks to help others succeed."

The analogy may sound naïve, but it contains a tremendously significant idea that led to a new development in the evolution of *jên,* namely, life force. If *jên* were merely something comparable to the feeling of pain in the case of illness, it would be nothing more than a state of mind. But what is in operation is not merely feeling, but the vital force, the dynamic element behind all life and production.

This idea of life or production (*shêng*) goes back to the *Book of Changes,* where it is declared, "The great virtue of Heaven and Earth is production." In the *Comprehensive Discussions in the White Tiger Hall,* productivity is ascribed even to *jên.* "The man of *jên* loves production," it says. But to make *jên* and production synonymous was definitely an innovation of the Neo-Confucianists. Chou Tun-i said, "To grow things is *jên.*" To Ch'êng Hao, "The will to grow in all things is most impressive. . . . This is *jên.*" And according to his brother, Ch'êng I, "The mind is like seeds. Their characteristic of growth is *jên.*" Even Hsieh Liang-tso said, "The seeds of peaches and apricots that can grow are called *jên.* It means that there is the will to grow. If we infer from this, we will understand what *jên* is." Such are the simple but direct expressions of the germinal idea which makes Confucian *jên* vital, dynamic, and life-giving. It is the exact antithesis of Buddhism and Taoism.

From the foregoing survey, we have seen that the concept of *jên* has gone through many stages of evolution and has grown more and more complex in meaning. From the original idea of *jên* as (1) kindness from above, it was broadened to mean (2) benevolence, still a particular virtue but no longer restricted to rulers, and further extended to connote (3) perfect virtue, which includes all particular virtues and applies to all men. In its application it was understood as (4) love, and, more specifically, (5) affection and, more emphatically, (6) universal love. On the psychological level, it is (7) man or (8) man's mind. Under the influence of Buddhism, it became (9) impartiality, which was in danger of becoming merely a state of mind, as was *jên* in terms of (10) consciousness, and so it was quickly modified as (11) impartiality embodied in the action of man. Finally, it was expanded to the limit to become (12) one body with the universe and the generative force of all things, namely, (13) process of production.

13

SPIRITUAL VALUES IN CONFUCIAN PHILOSOPHY

T'ang Chün-i

The Confucian school and the Taoist school are the main currents of thought of native Chinese philosophy. They and Buddhism have usually been mentioned together and called *"san-chiao,"* three teachings or three religions. Generally speaking, these three teachings all intend to deepen spiritual experience and cultivate the spiritual life of man, and have had much social-cultural influence on Chinese historical society. Hence, if we wish to know the main ideas of spiritual value in Chinese philosophy, we have to study them in the Confucian and Taoist and Buddhist philosophies.

It is held by some writers that there are no really spiritual values in Confucianism. It is said that in the body of Confucianism dealing with the virtues of men in definite relations only social values can be realized. Some contend that when Confucius talked about the importance of the cultivation of these virtues he always said this is a way for preserving the social solidarity of the nation or the peace of the world or for training the people to be contented with their circumstances and not to offend their superiors. These values are therefore alleged to be only socio-political and not spiritual values as defined

From "The Development of Ideas of Spiritual Value in Chinese Philosophy" by T'ang Chün-i, in *Philosophy and Culture East and West,* edited by Charles A. Moore (Honolulu: University of Hawaii Press, 1962), pp. 227–35.

Footnotes have been deleted.

above. Others contend that when Confucius talked about the values of the virtues he was considering the values as a means to the achieving of harmony and order in human relations, which were taken as a part of the harmony and order of the natural universe. But, the harmony and order of the natural universe may have a natural value only and not necessarily a spiritual value.

The views which efface the ideas of spiritual value from the Confucian ethical system are not without some justification. Actually, many Confucians in the course of Chinese history, such as those of the Yung-k'ang school and Yung-chia school of the Sung Dynasty (960–1279), and Yen Yüan (1635–1704) and Tai Chen (1723–1777) of the Ch'ing Dynasty (1644–1912), emphasized the social utilitarian value of ethical actions. Many Confucians in the Han Dynasty (206 B.C.–A.D. 220) emphasized the natural value of ethical action.

But the values of the virtues in Confucian ethics should be considered essentially spiritual values. The central idea of virtue peculiar to Confucius, Mencius (371–289? B.C.), and the Neo-Confucianism of the Sung-Ming period (960–1644) is to consider the virtues as the inner essence of one's personality, and their values as intrinsic to one's moral consciousness and tinged with a certain religious meaning, and thus as definitely spiritual values. The key concept in this interpretation is the concept of "searching in oneself," which is a teaching handed down from Confucius himself and developed by all later Confucians. I shall explain its meaning from three aspects.

(1) In the first aspect, "searching in oneself" means that in all ethical relations one has to do his duty to others, but not require others to do their duties to him, reciprocally, though the others should do their duties of their own accord. In order to explain this we have to know that there are three ways to develop one's spiritual life to the fullest extent, and all three may be called in a certain sense "backward" ways.

The first way is to get real freedom from all the instinctive and irrational desires in human life. The extreme of this is what Schopenhauer called the denial or mortification of the will. This way is practiced, more or less, by all ascetics and mystics, as a negative step in the very beginning of spiritual cultivation for higher positive spiritual development.

The second way searches for some kind of higher or highest Idea or Existence in the very beginning of spiritual cultivation which is supernatural and transcendent, such as the Idea of the Good in Plato and the self-existent God in the otherworldly religions. We may call this the way of leaving the mundane world behind, in our process of spiritual ascent.

The third way is to live in definite ethical relations with others in the actual world, practicing the morality of doing one's duty to others but not asking them to do their duties, reciprocally, as taught in Confucianism. This way of life may be called the way of thinking or acting morally just for oneself, which is opposite to the "forward way of asking others to do something morally for me," as in the common attitude of our daily life. It is a "backward" way of life and is as difficult to put into practice as the other two ways.

The difficulties of this third way arise from the fact that when one does his duty to others he naturally supposes that others are moral beings like himself. According to the universal principle of reason, man naturally expects others to do their duties in response to his action. Thus, he naturally thinks he has the right to demand that others do their duties. Actually, social justice and legislation are based upon the reciprocity of rights and duties. One who does his duty without asking others to do theirs is the same as one who has only duty-consciousness without rights-consciousness and lives beyond the idea of social justice. In duty-consciousness, one does what his conscience commands him to do, and never goes beyond his conscience to see what happens in other consciences, and so the value realized is completely internal to his conscience and is therefore a purely spiritual moral value. If I have this kind of duty-consciousness in full degree, then, the less others do their duty to me, the more I shall do my duty to others. That is to say, the more my expectation from others is disappointed, the more intensified is my self-expectation from myself. The value of social justice, which is offended and lost because others do not do their duty, is recompensed and satisfied by the moral values of my fulfillment, which is purely spiritual and belongs to my inward life. Yet, this kind of duty-consciousness is the most difficult for human beings, because we have to do to others more than they deserve. What we do to others is the same as the grace of deity conferred on man, though man may not be aware of it or respond to it with a sense of thanksgiving. It is significant that

Christians translate the word "grace" with the Chinese word *"en"* in the term *"en-i,"* which means that one does his duty without reciprocation, and so confers something which is absolutely beyond what others deserve. Therefore, we may say that in the first meaning of "searching in oneself" in Confucianism a deification of human life is implied and has religious and spiritual meanings.

(2) The second meaning of "searching in oneself" is that one ought to cultivate his virtues and abilities without asking praise from others. This is also very difficult to practice, due to the fact that men, motivated by the universal principle of reason, naturally want others to appreciate or approve what they themselves have appreciated or approved. This desire may not be morally bad, if it is accompanied by a moral feeling of respect when we request it from others and accompanied by our gratitude when we receive it from others. But, leaving the desire for praise itself alone and as unconditionally right, then we may simply take the praise of others as personal gratification. When we are anxious to receive this kind of gratification, many modes of moral evils, such as ambition, or the will to power to control the will of others, or disloyalty to one's original ideals in flattering others and then receiving praise in return, can be generated in different circumstances. When I ask the praise of others, I am taking my virtues and abilities, and their expressions in actions and speech, as a means, and they then have only instrumental or utilitarian value, which is non-spiritual social value or quasi-spiritual value . . .

If our ordinary outward desire of gaining others' praise is diminished, we may live a life which is directed by our moral conscience itself. We can then eradicate the roots of our desire to control the will of others; we will never be disloyal to the moral ideal in order to please men, and, at the same time, never have any complaint or grudge against others or Heaven. This is the meaning of the Confucian saying: "There is no one that knows me. . . . I do not murmur against Heaven. I do not grumble against men. . . . But it is Heaven that knows me." This is a kind of deified human life.

(3) The third meaning of "searching in oneself" is that all the moral principles, moral ideals, and moral values of our actions and intentions can be discovered by self-reflection. This is strongly implied in the teaching of Confucius, and is explicitly stated and elab-

orated in the teaching of Mencius and many later Confucians, as in the thesis that "human nature is good."

The thesis that "human nature is good" has had various interpretations in the various schools of Confucianism. In the teaching of Mencius, the first exponent of this thesis, the doctrine does not say that all actions or intentions of men are actually good enough. It says simply that there are good tendencies or good beginnings in human nature and, most important, that, when we have good intentions or do good actions, there is usually an accompanying feeling of self-satisfaction or self-joy or self-peace. This may be said to be deep self-praise when I find my intention or action is really good. This deep self-praise is usually concealed when we are eager to ask for praise from others or when we lack deep self-reflection. Yet, when we withdraw the desire to ask others for praise and have deep reflection, then everybody can find the deep self-praise which accompanies all good intentions or good actions. However, this deep self-praise is a result of my deepest self-evaluation, which immediately follows my intention or action. This self-evaluation reveals to me what is good as good and what is not good as not good, and from the former I feel self-satisfaction, self-joy, and self-peace, but from the latter I feel disquieted, unjoyful, and dissatisfied. As my mind feels self-peace or self-joy or self-satisfaction in the good only, so my human nature is disclosed as essentially good. This is the orthodox doctrine of the thesis that "human nature is good," which was morally expounded in Mencius' teaching, was metaphysically explained by Chu Hsi's (1130–1200) theory of *li* (principle, reason, or law), and culminated in the teaching of *liang-chih* (almost the same as conscience) in Wang Shou-jen's (Wang Yang-ming, 1472–1529) philosophy.

If we take human nature as essentially good, moral ideals and moral principles are nothing other than the norms or standards awakened within or originating in the nature of our mind and immanently presented to our moral self-consciousness for self-evaluation. Consequently, our moral training and moral cultivation have no other purpose than to preserve and extend what is judged or evaluated as good, and all the achievements of moral life and the formation of a moral personality express no more than the desire to conform to these immanent norms or standards, to realize what originates from the nature of the mind, and to know and to fulfill to the maximum what is implicitly contained in the nature of the mind.

However, in the development of our moral life, any phase of our ordinary life which is taken by common sense as non-moral or immoral can be evaluated as either good or evil. So, every phase of our life has moral meaning, can be made moral by a certain cultivation, and then has moral value, which can be presented immediately to our self-reflection, as defined above, and become a purely internal value. It is not difficult to see that if we resolve to have all the phases of our life made moral then our self-evaluations and self-reflections may arise successfully and co-extensively with the extensions of all phases of life, including those phases of our life which are considered by common sense as merely directing to, or dealing with, the so-called external environment.

Hence, self-evaluation and self-reflection should not be taken as subjective and self-closed, but should also be taken as objective and self-open to all the other social and natural objects of the universe as our whole environment. Here the "investigation of things" as taught by Confucianism has not only intellectual value but also moral value, and then we may have the wisdom that all the objects in the universe can be taken as the occasions for the realization of spiritual moral values, and that all may be lighted and permeated by spiritual and moral values as well. This is the vision of the moral man, who realizes his good nature, develops his moral life to the fullest extent, attains unity of the inner world and the outer world, and achieves the grandeur and beauty of personality as expounded in *The Doctrine of the Mean* and *The Book of Mencius*.

If we compare the thesis that human nature is good with the idea of original sin in Christianity or the *karma* theory and the *avidyā* theory of Buddhism, there are many pros and cons worthy of discussion. Yet, if we acknowledge the existence of original sin or impure *karma* in the depth of our mind, we may still believe that human nature is essentially good. We may hold that original sin and impure *karma* are not derived from real human nature, but that the feeling of unrest that arises when we are told we have original sin or impure *karma* originates from our real human nature. This nature, as revealed in unrest, is the same as the nature revealed in our unpeacefulness in our evils, and is absolutely good. In the feeling of unrest, of course, I may find at the same time that I am so weak as to try to set myself free from the bondage of original sin or impure *karma,* and I may pray to some transcendent being, such as God, *Brahman,* or Amida Buddha, to save me. In this type of religious consciousness, we think our nature is not good enough. Yet, the very confession of our weakness and our praying come from our nature, too. Our very confession may not be weak, and our praying must be good in itself. If it is objected that the very confession and words of prayer do not come from our human nature, but are the result of human nature as affected by a transcendent being or receiving grace from above, then we reply that our capacity for being (and our unconscious willingness to be) affected and receiving grace are additional evidences that human nature is essentially good. If we deny this, then how is it possible that men can be saved? The thesis that human nature is good does not fundamentally oppose the ultimate teachings of Christianity or Brāhmanism or Buddhism, which believe either that man is the image of God, or that man is *Brahman,* or that the Buddha is a sentient being awakened to the fullest extent. Therefore, the thesis that human nature is good cannot be denied, even if we concede the existence of original sin or impure *karma,* because we can reassert our nature as good again in the very self-reflection of our unrest or unpeacefulness in our evils and our very unwillingness to be bound by them. However, the Confucian thesis that human nature is good is still different from many religious points of view which take the evil origin of human actions much more seriously and believe that only a transcendent being can save man from evil. Men who hold the latter point of view always look at human nature as a mere potentiality and insist that the principle of its actuality resides in some transcendent being. Yet, from the thesis that human nature is good the principle of actualization is seen to be immanent in human nature.

What we have said above does not imply that Confucian thought lacks the idea of transcendent reality, such as God, the Mind of Heaven, or the Universal Mind. In fact, many Confucians have these ideas. The real difference between the Confucian point of view and the above religious point of view is that, in the latter, the idea of a transcendent being, such as God, *Brahman,* etc., is more easily brought to light by contrasting it with our sin or impure *karma* or bondage; while, in the former, the idea of the Mind of Heaven, the Universal Mind, God, or Heaven is usually brought to light by the positive development of our moral life to the fullest extent, with the knowledge that the transcendent being is at the same time immanent in our moral life. How is it possible to have these ideas brought to light by the positive development of our moral lives? The answer was suggested in the teaching of Mencius and culminated in the Neo-Confucians of the Sung-Ming period, who had a deep understanding of the thesis that human nature is good.

Briefly, the central theme of this trend of thought is that when we develop our moral life to the fullest extent, as a sage does, the essence of our good nature is wholly actualized in, presented to, and known by, our self-consciousness. The essence of our good nature may be said to be *jen,* which is love, beginning with filial piety, and flowing out as universal love to all the men with whom we have definite ethical relations, to all the people under Heaven, and to all natural things. So, the moral consciousness of *jen,* in its fullest extent, is all-embracing love, which pervades, permeates, and fills Heaven and Earth as a whole. So, Mencius said, "The virtuous man transforms all experiences he passes through and abides in holiness or deity-nature. His virtues are confluent with Heaven above and with Earth below." Chang Tsai (Chang Heng-ch'ü, 1020–1077), Ch'eng Hao (Ch'eng Ming-tao, 1032–1085), Ch'eng I (Ch'eng I-ch'uan, 1033–1107), and Chu Hsi had the same idea namely, that the man who realizes *jen* considers Heaven, Earth, and the ten thousand things as one body. Lu Chiu-yüan (Lu Hsiang-shan, 1139–1193) said, "The universe is my mind and my mind is the universe." Wang Shou-jen said, "Pervading Heaven and Earth is just this spiritual light—my spiritual light—which is not separated by, or separated from, Heaven, Earth, deities, and the ten thousand things." But is this mind only my own? In the mind which identifies itself with the universe, where is the dividing point between what is mine and what is not mine? When selfish ideas and motives are transformed into universal and all-pervading love, where is the borderline or the boundary between our mind and the universe? Why can I not take this type of mind as belonging to me and also to Heaven? Why can I not take this type of mind both as created and presented by myself and as revealed and descended to me from Heaven? Is its belonging-to-me incompatible with its belonging-to-Heaven? If I take this kind of mind as mine and not of Heaven, does this not simply contradict the very nature of this kind of mind, which has no borderline to differentiate itself from what is not itself and which is felt as a universal and all-pervading mind? Therefore, when I have this kind of mind and know its nature truly, I shall never take this mind merely as my own; I shall know that this kind of mind is conferred by Heaven as much as it is mine, and I shall know Heaven (which was originally synonymous with the word "God" in the Chinese Classics). As this kind of mind is the mind of one who develops his moral life to the fullest extent, and whose *jen* is wholly actualized as a sage, so the sage is said to be the same as Heaven, and human nature is therefore sometimes called Heaven-nature, and the human mind is called the mind of Heaven in some Confucian literature. So, Mencius said, "To have our mind preserved and Nature nourished is the way to serve Heaven" and "The man who has passed through the stage of completing his virtues and sheds forth his spiritual light brilliantly, and then can transform the world, is called a sage. The sage, unfathomable by intellect, is called holy or divine."

Yet, the highest teaching of Confucianism is not merely the realization that the sage is the same as Heaven, but the realization of the universal attainability of sagehood for all men and what is implied by that. The universal attainability of sagehood is a logical consequence of the belief that human nature is good. The sage is the man who has fully realized his nature. If all men have the same good human nature, surely all can realize their nature and attain sagehood. Furthermore, the universal attainability of sagehood is itself an immanent belief of the mind of the sage. Since the mind of the sage is full of love and unselfishness to the fullest extent, he could not have any idea that he is the only sage, because this is selfish and contradictory to the very nature of his mind. He must love to see, expect, and hope that everyone else will be a sage. Therefore, the universal attainability of sagehood is a belief immanently involved in the mind of the sage. If I believe there is a sage, or if I can be a sage, then I have to think of the idea of the sage through the mind of the sage, and thus the universal attainability of sagehood is also involved in my idea. Yet, according to the thesis that human nature is good, I must believe there is a sage and that I can be one, because sagehood is nothing more than my own nature, *jen,* wholly realized. So, I must believe in the universal attainability of sagehood.

According to the idea of the universal attainability of sagehood, an actual sage can be born at any time and any place in the world, and no one sage of any particular place or particular time has the privilege of being the only sage. As all sages have the same fundamental virtue, *jen,* or universal love, so all sages go in the same way, and are of the same spirit of mind, and live with the same principle or the same *Tao.* This idea led the Chinese people to believe that there can be sages in different religions of different peoples. This is one reason there were no religious wars or large-scale religious persecutions in Chinese history. So, this idea has its religious value.

Furthermore, when we know there is a single spirit, or a single mind, or a single principle, or a single *Tao* in the world of sages, we have to know one thing more. This is: "I can know all this in my here-and-now mind." This is to say that I can comprehend what is universal and all-pervading in the world of sages in my here-and-now mind. So, the world of sages is as much immanent in my here-and-now spiritual world as it is transcendent to my here-and-now actual existence. When I am awakened to this idea, then all that is remote, such as the highest ideals or holy virtues of sages, is nearest to my here-and-now mind, and all the values of the highest ideals and holy virtues belong to my mind as much as they do to the minds of sages themselves. This is perhaps the highest idea of human spiritual life expounded by the thinkers of the late Ming (1368–1644) after Wang Shou-jen. It is too subtle to explain all its meanings here.

14

THE MEANING OF TAO

Chung-yuan Chang

According to the Taoist tradition, the fundamental consideration of Tao is not epistomological but ontological. What is Tao itself? The only way we can get an answer is through our inner awareness in which our innermost being interfuses with the ultimate reality of all things. This inexpressible inner experience is illustrated in the analogy in which it is said: "You drink water and you know if it is warm or cold." In other words, Tao is conceived of as self-realization, a process of psychic integration, which, to be properly understood, requires long years of self-cultivation and cannot be conveyed verbally. Therefore, I will not concern myself today with a discussion of Tao as self-realization, but I will instead present to you the basic principles of Tao.

In our daily empirical life we are constantly drawing distinctions between things. They are high or low, long or short, black or white, yin or yang. These polarities are infinite in number. The Taoist would ask whether there is any possibility of finding unity within this diversity, and if so, in what way are these opposites related to each other? Chuang Tzu puts the problem thus: "because a thing is greater than other things, we call it great; therefore all things in the world have an opportunity to be great. Because a thing is smaller than other things, we call it small; therefore all things in the world

"The Meaning of Tao" by Chung-yuan Chang. From *Proceedings of the XIIth International Congress of Philosophy* 10 (1960): 33–40. Reprinted by permission of the author.

at same time might be called small." How, then, can we call a thing great or small? As a matter of fact, any measurement is relative, temporary, and constantly subject to change. One coin is said to be heavier than another coin, yet lighter than a third. Consequently, in reality the coin possesses the seemingly opposed qualities of heavy and light at the same time.

In his work, in the chapter "On the Identity of All Things," Chuang Tzu devotes himself entirely to expounding the unification and interfusion of all things. Chuang Tzu maintains that Tao is obscured by inadequate understanding, exemplified in the disagreement between the Confucian and Moist schools, each denying what the other affirms and affirming what the other denies. There is no real distinction between affirmation and negation, says Chuang Tzu. He goes on to say that "as soon as there is affirmation, there is negation; as soon as there is negation, there is affirmation. There is nothing which is not this, and there is nothing which is not that." Is there any real distinction between this and that, between affirmation and negation? When this and that are *not* placed in polar positions, we come to the central principle of Tao. Thus, according to Chuang Tzu's idea, if we understand that all measurements are relative and subject to change, and we are not confused by these arbitrary distinctions and determinations, we will then have the absolute freedom necessary to the achievement of Enlightenment.

It is interesting to note that in addition to the ontological concept of this process of identification, as described by Chuang Tzu, there emerges a latent logical process as well. The Taoists maintain that every assertion bears within itself its own opposite, so that when anything is asserted, its opposite necessarily is asserted at the same time. Lao Tzu explained in the second chapter of his book that when beauty is universally recognized as beauty, its opposite, ugliness, emerges. Similarly, when goodness is universally recognized, its opposite, evil, must appear too. Thus, being and non-being, easy and difficult, long and short, high and low, front and back, and other polarities are mutually produced by this logical process of transition. However, this transitional process does not only occur within polarities, but is, rather, a continuous sequence of negation and affirmation. As Chuang Tzu himself expounded in the second chapter of his work: "there is beginning, there is no beginning. There is no no-beginning. There is being, there is non-being. There is no non-being." This idea of logical transition was later developed in his book into a rough sketch of a theory of biological evolution. In chapter 18 of his work, we have the illustration of constant transition by tracing back the origin of living things from the germ to plants, from plants to animal creatures, with man finally emerging. Whether there is any real scientific contribution to the theory of evolution in his specific observations is not important here, but his illustration does indicate an awareness of the natural development of living things through the constant process of affirmation and negation.

This process of constant interaction was originally conceived by Lao Tzu as a creative net. As he says in chapter 42 of the *Tao Te Ching*: "from the Tao, One is created. From the One, Two; from the Two, Three; from the Three, Ten Thousand Things." The numbers as used here are simply to indicate the creative process of affirmation and negation.

For Taoists, nothing in nature exists isolated by itself. Rather, all things are interdependent. Thus, no phenomenon in nature can be truly understood by separating it from other things. However, the interaction of these things, as we have previously pointed out, is not limited to polar entities. Taoists also expound their organic concept of the unity of multiplicity, or Oneness, as it is often called. In chapter 25 of the work of Chuang Tzu, he says: "when we point to the different parts of the horse's body, we do not thereby have a horse. But when we conceive the integration of all parts of the body, then we have a horse in front of us." This organic concept of unity illustrates the formation of the whole through the interrelation of all the parts, that is, the discordant parts unite together to form a harmonious whole. When all parts unify themselves into an organic whole, each part breaks through its own shell and interfuses with every other part; each identifies itself with every other one. Thus, one is in many and many are in one. In this way, all particularities dissolve into one and all parts of the whole disappear into every other part in the whole. Each individual merges into every other individual; it is through this unity in multiplicity that the interfusion and identification of each individuality serves its function in the creation of the whole. This idea has been illustrated by Lao Tzu in chapter 11 of his book:

> Thirty spokes joined at the hub.
> From their non-being
> Comes the function of the wheel.
>
> Shape clay into a vessel.
> From its non-being
> Comes the function of the vessel.

The wheel is the unity of the spokes, and the vessel is the unity of the clay. In Lao Tzu's sense, the wheel can function as a wheel due to the organic relationships among the spokes. In other words, the interfusion and identification of the parts create a functioning whole.

The Taoists, however, did not stop there. They enlarged their organic concept into more metaphysical insights. As Chuang Tzu once said: "Heaven and Earth and I live together, and therein all things and I are one." This oneness is the product of his ontological awareness, which is invisible and unfathomable. This invisible and unfathomable oneness is called the realm of the Great Infinite. In the realm of the Great Infinite there is neither space nor time. It is, in fact, the realm of non-being which is absolutely free from limitations and distinctions. We have Chuang Tzu's own description of the realm of non-being: "Being is without dwelling place, continuity is without duration. Being without dwelling place is space, continuity without duration is time. There is birth, there is death; there is issuing forth, there is entering in. That through which one passes in and out without seeing its form—that is the Gate of Heaven. The Gate of Heaven is Non-Being. All things sprang from Non-Being." (c. 23) Non-Being is the higher unity of all things. It is the invisible and unfathomable Absolute Reality of all potentialities and possibilities of the universe. So Lao Tzu calls it the Great, which means infinite, boundless, and immeasurable. When we think of this immeasurableness, it gives us some sort of insight into the timelessness of time and the spacelessness of space. It is the absolute moment which opens the secret to the existence of all things, and frees us from previous rational conditioning and limitations. When Lao Tzu called Tao the "Mother of All Things," he referred to the realm of Non-Being as the primordial source of every beginning, the Absolute Reality from which all birth issues forth.

The Taoist organic concept has greatly influenced both Confucianism and Chinese Buddhism. As we know, *I Ching* or the *Book of Changes* is the product of the synthesis of Confucianism, the Yin-Yang school, and Taoist philosophy. The highest stage of "Unimpeded mutual solution" or "Shih Shih Yuan Yung Wu Ai" of the Hua Yen school of seventh century Buddhism has been related to Chuang Tzu's metaphysics by Chinese scholars. And later, the Neo-Confucianism of the eleventh century further developed the theory that "T'ai Chi" or "Ultimate" and "Li" or "Principle" are all related to this organic concept of the early Taoist. The basic organic concept of Taoist philosophy can be illustrated by the notion of creativity and sympathy. When all potentialities of the absolute realm of non-being or the infinite penetrates into every diversity, one embraces all particularities and enters into each. Such a process represents the Great Creativity. On the other hand, when all potentialities of every diversity unite into one, each particularity embraces all other particularities together penetrating into the realm of Non-Being. This process represents the activity of the Great Sympathy. From the point of view of sympathy, we see Tao as the synthesis of infinite possibilities and potentialities. This is the unity of particularities or multiplicities. From the point of view of Creativity, we see Tao as a radiative dispersion into infinite multiplicities and particularities. Thus, Creativity goes in the opposite direction from Sympathy. In short, Sympathy moves from all to One, Creativity moves from One to all. Without Sympathy there is no ground for fulfillment of potentialities to support Creativity. Without Creativity there is no means of actuality to reveal Sympathy. Sympathy and Creativity move together hand in hand. Each represents an aspect of the process between One and all, the fundamental phenomenon of Taoist organic philosophy.

The metaphysical structure of the Sympathy is the realm of Absolute Reality in which everything breaks through the shell of itself and interfuses with every other thing. All the multiplicities and diversities of the universe interpenetrate one another and enter into the realm of Absolute Reality. In the Taoist ideal community, man makes no artificial effort toward morality, but his self is merged with other selves and all other selves are in turn merged into his self. Neither the individual nor the group is consciously aware of or purposefully directed toward this. Chuang Tzu's description of this manner of living appears in chapter 12 of his work: "They loved one another without knowing that to do so was benevolence. They were sincere without knowing that this was loyalty. They kept their promises without knowing that to do so was to be in good faith. Thus their actions left no trace and we have no record of their affairs."

What Chuang Tzu means by "no trace" is an explanation of the character of identification in the realm of Non-Being. Men in the realm of Non-Being are those who did not lose their original nature. As he says further:

> in the days of perfect nature, men were quiet in their movements and serene in their looks. They lived together with birds and beasts without distinctions of kind. There was no difference between the gentleman and the common man. Being equally without knowledge, nothing came between them (ch. 9).

This world of perfect nature is a world of free interfusion and unification among men and between men and all things. Between all multiplicities and diversities there existed no boundaries. Men could work with men and all could share spontaneously. Each identified with the other and all lived together as one. Man lived an innocent and primitive life, yet there was no conceit nor selfishness. In this simplicity and purity we see the free movement of the reality of man. This we cannot expect in a world merely moral and intellectual, full of distinctions and differentiations. Only in the world of absolutely free identity does the Great Sympathy exist; the universal force which holds together man and man and all things.

When we regard the realm of Non-Being as the ontological basis for the fulfillment of the Great Sympathy, it is to see Tao as interfusion and identification of infinite potentialities and possibilities. Thus the realm of Non-Being serves as the unit of multiplicities and diversities. But when we approach Tao from the reverse direction, we see Tao as having penetrated into infinite multiplicity and into the manifold diversities of existence. Thus, it is the dispersion of potentialities and possibilities from universality to particularity, and the fulfillment of the process of the Great Creativity. In the process of creativity each particularity reveals the potentiality of all universalities. Kuo Hsiang of fourth century gives us an illustration of this concept: "a man is born but six feet tall. . . . However insignificant his body may be, it takes a whole universe to support it." To see the unity within multiplicity is to see infinite potentialities manifested in each particularity. This insight is the Taoist contribution to the understanding of creativity.

Chuang Tzu gives us an illustration of this idea in his example of the centipede. From the relative point of view, the insect, of course, does have its hundred or so different legs. But from the higher point of view, there is a unification of multiplicity. The coordinated movement of all the legs is a manifestation of unity. From this unity we see the centipede as a whole. All has penetrated into One. And the movement of all the legs is an interpretation of the One into all.

When One enters into all, One embraces all particularities and enters into each. Such a process represents the Great Creativity, which is supported by all the vitality of Sympathy. When creativity manifests itself, the potentialities of all the infinite particularities enter into each particularity. Lao Tzu says: "obtaining the One, Heaven was made clear. Obtaining the one, Earth was made stable. Obtaining the One, the Gods were made spiritual. Obtaining the One, the valley was made full. Obtaining the One, all things lived and grew." The One which is possessed by Heaven and Earth and Gods and all things is the same One, the Tao. In other words, they all embrace the same One, the Tao, and the same One, the Tao, embraces and pervades them all.

What I have said may seem to indicate that Tao is no different from mysticism. However, we must realize that Tao in its organic concept has been accepted by modern scientists. As Joseph Needham has stated in his work on *Science and Civilization in China*, Vol. II: "the unity of nature is the basic assumption of natural science." Alfred North Whitehead speaks of the transition from Newtonian cosmology to the new philosophy of organism, saying that modern physics has abandoned the idea of Hume's "simple location" and considers energy not as localized but pervading time and space. Inorganic atoms as well as living cells turn out to be highly organized centers of ceaseless activity. The influences of each entity stream away even into the utmost recesses of the universe. There is no mysterious underlying substratum. Thus the process of the interrelations of events around us is the primary reality, and all else is derivative from that. Whitehead clearly stated in his book *Science and the Modern World* that "this reality occurs in the history of thought under many names, the Absolute, Brahman, Order of Heaven . . ." The Order of Heaven is what we called the Tao. With this background in mind I believe we will better understand the essence of Tao.

15

THE BUDDHIST CONTRIBUTIONS TO NEO-CONFUCIANISM AND TAOISM

Kenneth Ch'en

NEO-CONFUCIANISM

As an intellectual movement Neo-Confucianism drew the attention of the educated Chinese away from Buddhism back to the Confucian classics. However, this Neo-Confucianism was influenced by Buddhism in more ways than one. The Indian religion had become so intimate a part of the intellectual make-up of the Chinese that it was impossible for the Sung thinkers to give up Buddhism entirely. While the Neo-Confucianists used terms found in the Confucian classics, they interpreted those terms in the light of the dominant Buddhist atmosphere, and the Neo-Confucian system would be incomprehensible to one not familiar with the prevailing Buddhist ideas of the age.

An example of this may be seen in Chang Tsai's extension of the meaning of jen to embrace all under heaven. It is more than likely that in this extension the Buddhist conceptions of the universality of life and the all-compassionate bodhisattva, ever ready to save all sentient beings, played a role.

Although the Neo-Confucian idealist Lu Hsiang-shan based his emphasis on the mind on the *Book of Mencius* and the *Great Learning,* one cannot escape the suspicion that he was influenced by Bud-

From *Buddhism in China: A Historical Survey* by Kenneth Ch'en (Princeton: Princeton University Press, 1964), Princeton Studies in History of Religions, pp. 471–76. Footnotes have been deleted.

dhist, especially Ch'an, tenets. Indeed, Lu and his chief disciple, Wang Yang-ming (1472–1529), of the Ming Dynasty, were accused by their opponents of being Buddhists in disguise, this in spite of the fact that in a letter to a friend Lu criticized Buddhism severely for its selfishness and negation of life. The Ch'an School, with its cardinal tenet that this mind is the Buddha and that this mind intuitively and instantly knows what is right and wrong without depending upon external sources, very likely influenced the thinking of Lu and Wang. It is interesting to note that the controversy which raged within Buddhist circles—that of gradual versus instantaneous enlightenment—found its counterpart in the discussions of the Neo-Confucians, with Chu Hsi representing the gradual rational approach and Lu Hsiang-shan the intuitive instantaneous approach.

In their advocacy of concentration of mind the Neo-Confucianists also appear to have been influenced by the Buddhists. Buddhist mental discipline emphasizes, among other things, mindfulness, meditation, and equanimity. Ch'eng Hao stressed these very things in his essay *Tranquility in Human Nature*. He wrote that tranquility means quietness in time of activity and inactivity, and that when the mind is excited, it becomes overactive and falls into uncertainty. He advocated concentrating the mind on one subject; when one does this, he said, the mind is its own master, will not fall prey to external influences, and cannot be harmed by any enemy.

From Li Ao to the Ch'eng brothers the Neo-Confucianists all had their say about what constituted sagehood. Li Ao wrote that a sage is enlightened when he is master of his emotions. Ch'eng Yi also wrote that the sage is one who controls his emotions of joy, anger, sorrow, fear, love, dislike, and greed, and adjusts his expression to the principle of the golden mean. This Confucian preoccupation with sagehood was probably a response to the Buddhist emphasis on the attainment of bodhisattvahood.

There were also particular views held by the Sung philosophers that might point to Buddhist influence. For instance, Chu Hsi held that any object contains within it the supreme undivided ultimate as well as the particularizing principle which gives the object its individual character. Such an idea is close to the Hua-yen doctrine of interpenetration and intermutuality, the all in one and the one in all. Shao Yung (1011–1077) in his cosmological speculations had a theory that at the end of an epoch, which he said spanned 129,600 years, the present world system would come to an end, to be replaced by another. Chu Hsi also shared in this view. Such an idea was alien to the Chinese and was undoubtedly influenced by the well-known Indian concept of aeons and recurring world systems.

While pointing out these influences of Buddhism upon Neo-Confucianism, we must not make the mistake of overestimating the extent of such influences. Though the Neo-Confucianists studied Buddhism and appropriated Buddhist ideas, the system which they constructed was distinctly Chinese in its emphasis on the reality of the phenomenal world, the importance of the individual, and the value of social relations and responsibilities. A fair verdict of history would therefore be that in this movement the Sung philosophers returned to their native Confucian traditions via some excursions into the path of the Buddha.

BUDDHIST INFLUENCE ON TAOISM

Neo-Confucianism was not the only system affected by Buddhism; Taoism was also subjected to its all-pervading influence. During the Han Dynasty Buddhism was able to gain a foothold on Chinese soil by allying itself closely with Taoism and borrowing from it, but in later centuries it was the Taoist turn to borrow from Buddhism.

To begin with, the Taoists never had any idea of their system as a religion consisting of a body of doctrines and beliefs left behind by a master and preserved in a corpus of literature. It was only after Buddhism had come in and gained widespread acceptance that the Taoists took over from the Buddhists the idea of a religion. Once having made this initial appropriation, the Taoists decided that they might just as well go all the way in imitating the foreign model.

First, the Taoists themselves admitted that they borrowed the practice of making statues and images from the Buddhists. The first Taoist images of their deities appeared about the middle of the fifth century under the Northern Wei Dynasty, with the deities flanked on both sides by Taoist saints.

It is in the field of literature that the Buddhist contribution to Taoism is most obvious. In the early stages of Taoism as a religion it was a relatively simple matter for the Taoists to build up a body of literature of their own. All they had to do was to group together those works branded as heterodox by the Confucians—works on alchemy, divination, hygiene, breathing exercises, and so forth—and attribute these to the founder of their religion, Lao-tzu. However, there was a limit to the supply of such literature and the Taoists would have faced a prolonged drought if no other sources had been forthcoming. Meanwhile, the Buddhist sutras were flowing into China in a never-ending stream, inciting the envy of the Taoists with their variety, scope, and imagination. To the latter this was an inexhaustible supply from which they could borrow and copy—exactly what the Taoists did from the fifth century on. So hasty and slipshod was this wholesale copying that the Taoists left behind numerous traces of their unethical practice. In general it seemed that what the Taoist did was to take over a Buddhist sutra and then substitute Lao-tzu for the word Buddha whenever it appeared, but very often the copyist was not attentive enough to make all the changes. Consequently, in some of the so-called Taoist works, we find such passages as the following:

> Of all the teachings in the world, the Buddha's teaching is foremost (*Hsi-sheng ching, Sutra on the Western Ascent*).
>
> Our master is called the Buddha, who follows the incomparable teaching (*Wen-shih-chuan, Biography of Wen-shih*).
>
> The host of saints and immortals have already realized the way of the Buddha (*Tung-hsüan chen-i ching, Sutra on the True Unity Which Penetrates Mystery*).

The most obvious of such borrowings may be seen in the biographies of Lao-tzu that appeared during the Sung Dynasty. In one of these biographies, the *Yu-lung-chuan* (*Biography of the One Who Resembles a Dragon*), we read that Lao-tzu was born by issuing forth from the left rib of the Holy Mother, who was clinging to the branches of the plum tree at the time. As soon as he was born, he took nine steps and from each footprint lotus flowers sprang forth. At the time of his birth ten thousand cranes hovered above in the skies, while nine dragons spat forth water to bathe the newborn baby. After he was born, with his left hand pointing to heaven and his right hand to earth, he uttered the cry that in heaven and earth only the Tao was supreme. Nine days after birth his body become endowed with the seventy-two major and eighty-one minor characteristics. The Holy Mother, after giving birth to Lao-tzu, then mounted a jade chariot and in broad daylight ascended to heaven.

It is perfectly clear that such a biography of Lao-tzu was nothing more than a retouching of a Buddhist source, very likely the *Lalitavistara,* with some changes in proper names here and there.

Having built up their body of literature, the Taoists then organized it into a canon modeled, as one would expect, after the Buddhist Tripitaka. Consequently, the Taoist canon now consists of three sections, with each section then divided into twelve categories.

Certain concepts of the Buddhists were also taken over by the Taoists. An example of this was the concept of the bodies of the Buddha. During the Period of Disunity the Taoists had already developed the idea that the supreme Tao, in order to instruct deities and men in the world, from time to time would assume a human form to perform this function. The historic Lao-tzu was but one of these incarnations. Such a Taoist idea was undoubtedly based on the Buddhist doctrine of the two bodies of the Buddha, the *dharmakāya* or the body of essence, which is the only true and real body of the Lord, and the *nirmānakāya* or body of transformation, which is the manifestation of the *dharmakāya* on earth. In imitation of the bodhisattva, the all-loving and compassionate being, the Taoists brought forth a class of transcendent beings called *t'ien-tsun,* venerable celestials, conceived of chiefly as instructors and saviors. One of these celestials was said to have been eternally teaching and converting people since the beginning of time. The Buddhist concepts of karma and rebirth were likewise appropriated, as indicated in the following passage:

> The Taoist saints since countless aeons in the past . . . have all depended on the merits of their past lives to attain to the Tao of the present; they have without exception reached their present state through the accumulation of merits derived from their former careers. . . .

This is in contrast with the earlier Taoist doctrine of the transmission of burden, according to which the merits and demerits accrued by an individual were manifested not in his future lives but were passed on to descendants of later generations. Finally, the Buddhist concept of the three worlds—the world of desires, the world of forms, and the formless world—was taken over *in toto* by the Taoists.

This brief summary will suffice to show how much the Taoists appropriated from the Buddhists in their views on cosmology, pantheon, literature, and doctrines. Instead of Taoism's swallowing up Buddhism, as was feared at the end of the Han Dynasty, the Taoists were themselves overwhelmed by the Buddhists.

16

RELIGIONS IN THIRTEENTH-CENTURY CHINA

Jacques Gernet

GENERAL CONCEPTS

Nothing could be more diversified than the religious aspects of Chinese life in the thirteenth century. Yet at the risk of oversimplification, an attempt must first and foremost be made to define the spirit which animated religious life as a whole. It must at once be admitted that it contained nothing in the nature of what we Western people of today would call religious sentiment. That is to say, that any kind of dialogue between Man and God, or mystical outpourings addressed to a personal deity, are entirely foreign to it. In so far as its specifically Chinese character is concerned, religious life seems to have been dominated by a sort of latent and unexpressed obsession: that of the possibility of cosmic disorder. That the seas might take the place of the mountains, that the seasons might no longer follow their natural sequence, that Heaven, and Earth might be confounded—these were the kind of apocalyptically unnatural happenings that the ceremonies of the various cults were designed to avert.

The aim of most religious acts was either to regulate Space, to keep it literally in place—and the tutelary mountains, covered by

From *Daily Life in China in the Thirteenth Century* by Jacques Gernet, translated by H. M. Wright (New York: The Macmillan Company, 1962), pp. 197–215. Copyright, 1962, by George Allen and Unwin Ltd. Reprinted by permission of The Macmillan Company and George Allen and Unwin Ltd. Footnotes have been deleted.

sanctuaries both official and private, saw to this; or to regulate Time, inaugurate it, renew it—and the annual festivals helped to ensure its constant renewal; because of them, the world was never more than one year old. From any point throughout the whole of nature —mountains, hills, rivers, streams, rocks and trees—emanations could come forth which might be good or bad, propitious or unpropitious. The main purposes of ancestral graves and of the sanctuaries dedicated to ancestors, to deified historical personages, and to the innumerable deities borrowed from the Buddhist or the Taoist pantheons, seems to have been to provide a focus for good influences that would be of benefit to man, while in themselves they gave rise to beneficent emanations. The natural and the supernatural intermingled.

Each deity had a specific region which it protected: such-and-such a town, district, village or house; and its cult was a guarantee against ills of all kinds that might sweep down upon humankind: wars, floods, droughts, epidemics, fires . . . The official cult performed by the Emperor and the ordinary family cult were essentially the same. A grave in the right situation might have just as fortunate an effect on the destinies of a family as the judicious choice of a holy mountain might have on a whole region of the empire. But there were also gods for special purposes. They were called upon for protection against this or that particular scourge, or in the hope of making a fortune, or of having male descendants, or of succeeding in the official examinations . . . It was also possible to get useful information from the gods of certain sanctuaries. Candidates for the examinations slept in temples so as to have premonitory dreams; judges sometimes did the same when they felt the need for divine inspiration in order to discover who the guilty party was.

But it was local powers and local gods that were the main concern, and the most delicate problem of all was that of finding the most propitious spot for erecting a sanctuary. For any change made in the natural order of things might have grave consequences and demanded the taking of precautions. No house, no wall of a town, no temple was ever built, no grave dug, without some sort of certitude that such an act would have nothing but lucky effects. In order to choose such spots, specialists were consulted—soothsayers known as "geomancers," who made use of the compass and of complicated tables of correspondences, and possibly of their flair as well. However, even when every precaution had been taken, the result sometimes fell short of perfection. Thus, at Ch'eng-tu, where the marking-out of the city walls had been done in accordance with indications given by the ancient method of divination by means of the shell of a tortoise, topography had also had to be taken into account. So, since the ramparts had been built on a steep hill, it was thought advisable to erect a pavilion 90 feet high "in order to fix the North and the South." The excavation of tombs, because it disturbed nature and death, was considered to be a particularly sacrilegious act. One man who had made a habit of excavating ancient tombs in order to find antique objects (and let us remember that antiques were all the rage in the Sung period) lost his memory in his old age. He could no longer recognize even the simplest written characters.

The divine was so little personalized, so *natural* as it were, that religious beliefs and practices seemed to express a lay conception of the world rather than that duality between the sacred and the profane that is so familiar to us and that seems to us essential to all religion. To know the auspicious seasons, days, orientations, places, colours, numbers and names—this was the secret for performing all actions that impinged upon the supernatural, for all things in the universe were in correspondence with each other. Portents already *were* the future, names called forth the realities they invoked. Great trouble was taken to choose propitious names and to avoid unpropitious ones. To the south of Chiu-chiang, on the shores of Lake P'u-yang, there was a mountain called the "Peak of the Twin Swords." The people of that region thought that the name was unlucky and that this was why the region was ravaged by wars every two hundred years. For a long time, says an author in 1177, the old men of the town had hoped that the name might be changed, but they had not been able to decide on their choice of a new one. There was no distinction made between the natural or supernatural powers inherent in things and creatures, and the things and creatures themselves. Nothing would be more absurd than to describe the religious thought of the Chinese by the term "animism."

These were the main features of religious life in general; but they do not provide a complete picture, for since the beginning of the Christian era China had gradually become permeated by notions of moral responsibility, compassion, and a saviour god. These ideas came from the West, either by sea, or via the caravans of Central Asia. However, this contribution of new ideas made no vital change in the Chinese genius. It became amalgamated without difficulty with autochthonous practices and beliefs: Buddhism, the great religion responsible for this enrichment, had to adapt itself to the exigencies of the Chinese way of thinking.

Another qualification should be added to the general indications which have been given. Although the more widely practised forms of religion were limited to the cult of local deities who ensured the prosperity of certain defined localities, there also existed among the people sects and secret societies animated by revolutionary and messianic hopes. These provided an aspect of religious life in China which was outside the main tradition, and which was "Dionysic" and prophetic. Fasting, trance and ecstasy were employed as a direct means of communication with the divine. It would be wrong to suppose that the most violent and extreme forms of religious sentiment were unknown. It all depended on the nature of the social surroundings and on local loyalties. For this reason it is important to distinguish between the official cult and the various popular cults, and between the forms taken by religion among the upper classes and those among the common people.

THE OFFICIAL CULT

The official cult as observed by the Emperor, who was its principal officiant, could be described as Confucianist in so far as it was inspired by traditional conceptions peculiar to the ruling class. It was addressed to Heaven, Earth, and the imperial ancestors. Its purpose was to ensure the continuity of the dynasty, to regulate Time and Space, and to give the world prosperity and peace. In addition to the annual rites which were fixed according to the solar calendar (the festivals for the solstices and for the beginning of the seasons), there were also special ceremonies, such as announcements made in the Supreme Temple (for example, of the inauguration of a new reign-period, of the death of a member of the imperial family, or of a public calamity), and sacrifices to Heaven and Earth on the altar in the southern suburbs.

One example will suffice to illustrate the characteristic features of the cult: its ritualism, the complexity of its regulations (numbers, colours, orientations, dates, etc. were all determined with respect to their symbolic meaning by specialists in ritual), and the ostentation of its ceremonies. The rites of the imperial cult were first and foremost grandiose spectacles, although these spectacles did not exclude a certain amount of religious emotion. All these traits will emerge from a description of one of the most important rites of the imperial cult—that of the sacrifices on the altar in the southern suburbs.

This altar was situated about fifteen hundred yards outside the Great Processional Gate on the southern ramparts. Its shape and dimensions had remained unaltered for several centuries. About thirty feet high, it was approached by a stairway of seventy-two steps in nine groups of eight, and was on four different levels, not including the top platform. Twelve steps led to this topmost level, which was twenty-one yards wide. On this platform there was a place for libations to the Emperor-on-High (Heaven) and two places for libations to the August Earth, as well as places for offerings made to the first emperors of the dynasty. Sixteen niches in the uppermost of the altar's four levels were used for the sacrifices to the mythical emperors of the five colours, to the planets, and to the 360 stars.

It was at this altar that the Emperor performed the ordinary rites such as those on the day of the beginning of spring, which fell about February 5th, or at the winter solstice, or when prayers were made for rain in times of drought. But there was also a special ceremony held there every three years. The imperial decree announcing the date fixed for it was issued on the first day of the year, and it was held either at the winter solstice of that year, or on the first day of the following year. A day in the 5th or 6th moon was chosen on which orders were given to the official services concerned to start preparing the altar and the lustration halls. These were constructions which had a framework of wood and bamboo covered over with matting and screened with green hangings. Soldiers were given the task of levelling the surface of the Imperial Way on the stretch leading from the Supreme Temple (the temple of the imperial ancestors) north of the palace to the altar in the southern suburbs, and then covering it with fine sand. A large temporary building was erected in front of the Supreme Temple in which to place the ceremonial chariot of the Emperor; the townspeople were allowed to come and see it.

During the month before the sacrifices, in the 12th or at the end of the 11th moon, rehearsals of the ceremony were held almost every day. Three days before it, the Emperor was bidden to purify himself by fasting in the "Hall of Great Fame." For this he donned the "hat of communication with Heaven," a tunic of fine silk, and various pendants. The following day, wearing a different kind of hat, he visited the "Hall of Bright Holiness," and returned from there to the Supreme Temple and then spent the night in one of the lustration halls. At the fourth beat of the drum, just before dawn, he donned his ceremonial headgear and went to sacrifice to his ancestors. During the night, soldiers provided with torches and bearing the imperial insignia were posted on both sides of the great avenue along the whole length of the Emperor's route from the Supreme Temple right to the altar for the sacrifices to Heaven. There were so many torches that it was like daylight. High officials, members of the imperial family and of wealthy and titled families were crowded in serried ranks.

When the Emperor mounted his chariot, all lights except those lining the route were extinguished. The imperial procession, led by tame elephants, now came out through the Great Processional Gate and made its way to the altar, near which a host of standards and flags flew. The sound of the imperial guards shouting orders to each other could be heard, and the flicker of torches could be seen against the daybreak. The earth shook with the beat of drums and the solemn sound of trumpets as an immense and silent crowd stood waiting on the open space at the foot of the altar. The court musicians played the ritual music. The Emperor mounted the altar steps, which were covered with yellow gauze (yellow being the colour of the centre and of sovereignty) and sprinkled with pieces of camphor. A victim was sacrified on the small adjacent altar to the God of the Soil, and then the Emperor, having reached the topmost platform of the altar for the sacrifices to Heaven, offered libations to Heaven, to the August Earth, and finally to his ancestors. To the last, he presented jade tablets along with the ritual wine. He read aloud what was written on these sacred tablets, which were afterwards desposited in the interior of the altar. Then he drank the "wine of happiness," and, when all was over, he made his way to the buildings that had been erected near the altar in order to change his robes. The officials offered their congratulations. Finally he mounted a ceremonial chariot, different from the one which had brought him to the sacrificial altar. A crowd of horsemen and of people on foot, made up of people from all ranks in society, followed the procession as far as the imperial palace.

This example shows how the official cult was at the same time formalistic in detail and spectacular in its general manifestation. It was a cult which was ideally suited to the requirements of the scholar-officials, who traditionally had always attached great importance to the rites, to their symbolic significance, their religious effects, and resulting psychological repercussions. They were people such as Montaigne described as being *"plus cérémonieux que dévotieux"* (ceremonious rather than devout). Indeed, religion, in the eyes of the scholars, had nothing to do with satisfying the mystical leanings of individuals; its aim was to ensure the preservation of a universal order which was nothing other than the counterpart, on the supernatural level, of the political order imposed upon the world by the Emperor and his officials. This accounted for the frequent hostility on the part of the scholars towards any form of religious sentiment which deviated from what they considered to be the norm. It also accounted for the need constantly felt by the rulers to regulate all aspects of the religious life of the empire and integrate them into the framework of the official religion. The chief holy places in the provinces were carefully graded and inscribed on the list of official sacrifices below the altars and temples of the capital where the most important ceremonies of the imperial cult were performed. This was an attempt on the part of the central power to annexe to itself the power exercised by local religious centres and at the same time to maintain control over the big popular cults.

The order of importance was as follows: the altar for the sacrifices to Heaven in the southern suburbs, the temple of the imperial ancestors, the imperial god-of-the-soil altar and the altar to Prince Millet, regional deities (sacred mountains, seas and lakes), ancient Sages and deified heroes. All these deities received official titles from the Emperor, and the determination of their names, which were graded not only according to the terms employed, but also to the number of written characters of which they were composed, was one of the sovereign's most important tasks. Thus, the god of the ramparts, a popular deity, received official offerings in the event of droughts, floods and epidemics. At Hangchow, this god has his temple on one of the hills to the south of the city. He was known as "Eternal Solidity," but had also received from the Emperor a longer and more pompous title.

This formalistic and "administrative" conception of religion was not far from being the equivalent of a complete lack of religious belief. At least a compromise could easily be arrived at between the two, and indeed there existed a rationalist tradition among the scholars which went very far back, one of its earliest representatives being Hsün-tzu, in the third century B.C. "If," said this unbelieving philosopher, "people pray for rain and get rain, why is this? I answer: There is no reason for it. If people do not pray for rain, it will nevertheless rain." But it may be noted that it was usually popular superstitions for which the scholar-officials reserved their ironical contempt. Some who were over-zealous as administrators even went to the length of demolishing local sanctuaries and cutting down sacred trees. But most of them had the sense to abstain from sacrilege of this kind for fear of the peasants' reactions.

The rationalism of the scholars was tempered with tolerance, and repressive measures were usually only directed against secret societies and against cults with political implications which threatened to be serious. As for Buddhism, which formerly, because of its influence and wealth, had aroused strong anticlerical feelings in T'ang times and earlier, it still drew sarcastic remarks from the scholars in Sung times. Their hostility had no doubt lost some of its violence along with the decline in political and economic power of the Buddhist communities, but the intellectual antipathy remained, and their disapproval had even become accentuated on the ideological plane. As many an anecdote testifies, it was the thing, in certain upper-class circles, to be anti-Buddhist. A guest of the celebrated eleventh-century writer Ou-yang Hsiu, having just learnt that one of the children in the family was called *Brother Monk,* expressed his astonishment. "How," he said jokingly to the great scholar, "how could you have given such a name to your son, you whose feelings about Buddhism are so well known?"—"But," replied the other, laughing, "is it not customary in order to protect children as they grow up [i.e., to keep off the evil eye] to give them childhood names that are despicable, such as *dog, sheep, horse?*"

Sometimes the scoffing took a turn of arguing the matter out. "After the death of a near relation," says one author,

> the Buddhist laity hold funeral services every seven days until the forty-ninth day after the death. They believe that if they act in this way, the sins of the deceased will be abolished, and that if they did not, the dead would go to hell and suffer horrible tortures. Now, after death, the body decays and the spirit dissipates in the air. How, then, can the dead suffer tortures?

"If there is neither paradise nor hell," says another,

> then that is that. If paradise exists, then it is to be expected that good people will be re-born there. If hells exist, it is only just that bad people should be thrown into them. It therefore follows that to address prayers to the Buddha on behalf of one's deceased parents is to regard one's father and mother as scoundrels and good-for-nothings.

This opposition to Buddhism on the part of the scholars was for the most part merely a matter of individual belief. In actual fact, the official cult did not scorn appealing occasionally to Buddhist deities for their support. If, from our point of view, this appears illogical, that is only because the religious sphere in the West is divided into separate doctrines with well-defined tenets and beliefs. In China, however, differences in doctrine were never of any importance. The only religious differences were differences of social context: official cult, family religion, local, regional or village cults, or professional ones in the case of the guilds; and in all these contexts, doctrine played a subordinate rôle.

The Buddhist and Taoist communities, which were in command of wealth derived from offerings and from the grants bestowed on monasteries in recognition of their official status, were commanded by the court to hold religious services on behalf of the Emperor, his ancestors, his close kin and his dynasty. "In this vast empire" wrote, in 1326, the bishop of Zaytun (Ch'üan-chou), André de Pérouse, "where there are people of all nations under heaven and of all sects, every single person is authorized to live according to his own sect, for they are imbued with the idea, or rather, the error, that everyone can find salvation according to his own sect." This general indifference towards doctrine was stronger still in the cults and beliefs of the people, because often a multitude of heterogeneous elements were quite indistinguishably intermingled in them.

FAMILY CULTS

The purpose of the ancestral cult was to create an intimate link between deceased parents—and in particular the most important among them, such as heads of clans and of lineages—and the events of family life such as New Year festivals, births, marriages, etc. Associated with this cult was the idea of a destiny and an individuality belonging to each family. It was a cult common to all classes of society, but which tended to become more important among families with illustrious forbears, and we have seen how that of the imperial ancestors, because of its political significance, occupied an important place in the official cult. The Emperor had his ancestral temple, the great families sanctuaries of a more modest nature, and ordinary people contented themselves with setting up a little altar in the main room of their house. On the ancestral altars were placed the tablets bearing the names of deceased parents, in which the ancestral spirits were supposed to reside. An effort was made to capture and fix these spirits at the moment of death, when, to give life to the tablets, marks were made on them with little spots of sacrificial blood, signifying the eyes and ears of the deceased. But the deceased were also still present in their graves, and at the Festival of the Dead on the 15th of the 7th moon (April 5th), and on the 1st of the 10th moon, pious kinsmen of all who had not been cremated came to sweep and water the graves of their close kin.

But the ancestors were not the only household deities. The gods of the door, of the hearth, of the bed, of the courtyard, of the well, of the earth, each received small offerings at New Year. The images of the door gods were renewed, and the god of the hearth was treated with greater respect than usual before making his journey to report in Heaven on the conduct of each member of the family. Each of these household gods had certain definite functions—for instance, the god of the bed was responsible for the fecundity of the couple—

and appeal was made to them during the course of the year if need be. They were by no means all-powerful gods (for that matter, no Chinese gods were); on the contrary, they were obliging and not at all vindictive, and could be spoken to on equal terms. As well as these, there were other gods, both Chinese and Buddhist, that could be invoked on the many occasions when petty troubles or distressing events came to disturb the happiness or the tranquillity of the family: wives might be sterile, or, contrary to the wishes of the family, be unable to give birth to anything but girls; confinements were sometimes difficult; daughters of the house clumsy and unable to sew or embroider; children sickly; illness, poverty or death might visit the house. The gods to whom the family presented their offerings had no other function but to protect them against these various misfortunes.

POPULAR CULTS AND BELIEFS

The household gods upon which the happiness of each family depended were not radically different from the protective deities of urban and rural communities. With them also the essential characteristic of the cult was that it was local and practised for the benefit of a group. Popular deities were innumerable: ancient sages, great poets, warrior heroes, gods with names borrowed from the Taoist pantheon, illustrious monks, great Buddhist saints and deities, gods of the soil and gods of the ramparts were worshipped in a multitude of sanctuaries and temples. Their powers even merged with those emanating from the earth and from the waters. There were certain trees, certain rocks, rivers and mountains that were supposed to have an influence on the course of the seasons, and the people also built sanctuaries in honour of these nature deities.

Sometimes local communities performed rites which were not part of an organized cult. In one place, a rock of peculiar form might be ceremonially whipped at times of prolonged rain or drought; in another, women's worn-out shoes and dead pigs might be thrown into a deep pool when its presiding spirit, a divine dragon, refused to put an end to a period of drought. On the other hand, the most important deities had their feast-days which, in the country, were at the same time days when fairs were held. Theatrical representations with clowns, jugglers and musicians were held in their honour. Requests for good harvest were addressed to them, and they were appealed to, on other days of the year, when a calamity threatened the village or the district: rains or dry weather which endangered the crops, floods, epidemics, etc. This is the first aspect of popular religion that strikes one: the extraordinary proliferation of gods.

But there are other and less well-known aspects that merit attention. Local gods were sometimes associated with spiritualistic practices. Mediums, visionaries and prophets in fact abounded among the people. Holiness and the gift of prophecy were usually incarnated in the most contemptible of creatures. Madmen, idiots, beggars in rags or poverty-stricken pedlars might be the incarnation of Chinese or Buddhist deities. Others claimed at least to be inspired by the gods and could evoke the souls of the illustrious dead and predict the future by means of riddles. Not only the common people, but sometimes also people from the upper classes and even certain emperors (for the central power liked to be surrounded with mystery and did not neglect magical aid) had faith in the ravings of such visionaries. One of them, a man called Sun the fishmonger, was summoned to the court in 1125, just before the barbarian invasion, and was housed in one of the imperial apartments. One day, the Emperor, emerging tired and starving with hunger from a long ceremony, saw Sun the fishmonger seated in the doorway of a small room with a steamed pancake held in his hand. "Have a bite," said the prophet, putting his pancake under the Emperor's nose. Then, seeing a look of incomprehension on the face of his illustrious interlocutor: "A day will come when you will be glad to have even a pancake like this." The following year the barbarians took the capital by storm and led the Emperor and his suite into captivity in the Manchurian desert.

However, mediums and prophets had the opportunity of employing their gifts more efficaciously within the framework of the secret societies. The state of trance could then become collective, aided by under-nourishment, alcohol, ecstatic dances, sexual practices of a magical nature, or fasts which sometimes reached a pitch of self-mutilation.

As might be expected, we are very ignorant about these secret societies. But when the government succeeded in exterminating one of them, it sometimes happened that contemporaries left some account of its organization and practices. Thus an author of the first half of the twelfth century gives us fairly precise information about a secret society of Manichean inspiration known as the Demon Worshippers that was very popular at that period. The new religion arose in Fukien and spread rapidly to the prefecture of Wen-chou and along the coast of southern Chekiang, and finally affected the whole province as far as the Yangtze. The sect, directed by an individual known as the Demon King with the aid of two assessors called the Demon Father and the Demon Mother, practised a kind of communism of ownership. New adepts were given free lodging and food, but they had to swear terrible oaths not to reveal the names of their associates and not to violate the interdicts of their sect. Contrary to the actual practices of Buddhists, the prohibitions against meat and alcohol were strictly observed, and violation of them entailed the confiscation of the property of the guilty person, half of which was assigned to those who had denounced him, and half to the officials set up by the sect in the districts where the rebellion had succeeded in ousting the imperial administrators.

Here is an instance which demonstrates the passionate ferocity with which the Demon Worshippers adhered to the tenets of their society. The patron saint of the sect had the name of Chiang Chiao. Hence the word *chiao,* which means "horn," was taboo for the faithful, and nothing, not even the most frightful tortures, would have made it escape their lips. So the prefect of T'ai-chou, in Chekiang, owing to the fact that he knew about this taboo, was able to identify the Demon Worshippers in this manner: on showing them a ram's horn, he could not get them to say the forbidden word. The sect proscribed the worship of all Chinese and Buddhist deities as well as the ancestral cult, and the only gods they recognized were the sun and the moon, which they considered to be "true Buddhas." Their funeral ceremonies were accompanied by a curious custom. On each side of the corpse, which was dressed and capped according to the rites customary throughout China, squatted two members of the society. "Will you have a cap in the next world?" says one. "No," says the other, upon which they remove the corpse's headgear. They continue in this way until the corpse is completely naked. "What will you have in the other world?" then say the two cronies. "You will have the sheath of a foetus," and they wrap it up in a sack of coarse cloth. This economical funeral fashion, together with the prohibitions against meat and alcohol and against holding banquets, provided, in the opinion of members of the sect, an excellent way of getting rich.

Like Buddhism, the new religion proclaimed that life was nothing but suffering, but they maintained that death itself brought final liberation. Hence to slay one's heretical neighbour was to ensure his salvation, and those members of the sect who had many murders to their credit had some chance of becoming Buddhas.

The regular cults with their public ceremonies, and the secret societies with their doctrines of personal salvation combined with messianic revolutionary tendencies, represented two sharply distinct and almost contradictory aspects of the religious life of the people. But this by no means exhausts the question of popular beliefs. For while the deities of the local sanctuaries were, for the ordinary person, the powers, either natural or but feebly personified, that ruled over their world, which was restricted to the locality and the group living in it, on another level, no longer that of collective practices but of traditional beliefs, the whole universe was peopled by spirits, genies, demons and ghosts.

Some of these were fantastic creatures in animal or human form, others were dogs, pigs, or foxes changed into men or sometimes into women of extraordinary beauty, others again were simply ghosts who had not received offerings or whose murder had not been avenged. How were unwelcome visitors such as these to be got rid of? The sound of firecrackers, drums and gongs chased them away. One could also strike them with a stick or a sword when one saw them. They then either regained their original form or disappeared. Willow branches or peach branches or artemisia scared away demons and pestilences. A high official passing through a market town in Szechwan at the time of the weaving of hemp noted in his travel diary that the inhabitants burnt artemisia in front of their doors in order to keep away evil influences. Other methods using symbols were found effective: designs of ramparts and moats, shields and halberds, designs using magic written characters. Another method advised was to place objects which demons disliked in their path—

for example, white jade, for demons, being female, like the dark and have a horror of the colour white. Conversely, there were certain acts that should be avoided. For instance, in Ch'eng-tu, in Szechwan, the drum was no longer beaten to sound the evening hours during the Sung period, because formerly it was at these hours that beheadings had taken place, and to sound the hours would awake the malevolent ghosts of the criminals whose bodies had been buried in the polo field.

All evil spirits who were chased away or identified by magic means usually only haunted either families or individuals. They formed a class of supernatural beings of an entirely different nature from that of the deities of the temples and local sanctuaries. Sorcerers, Taoist monks, and sometimes Buddhist monks, were the people who could exorcise these demons, either because of their knowledge of efficacious formulae, or because of the power derived from their religion.

Numerous anecdotes testify to the very widespread belief in a world of the dead and in the existence of an infernal court of justice presided over by the king of the lower regions. Some of the judges in this tribunal were former high officials, and the complex administration by which the world of the dead was ruled was a reproduction of that in the world of the living. The officials of the infernal regions had a career in the other world. They could be promoted and degraded, and they had under them a crowd of petty employees, archivists, scribes and guards. It sometimes happened that this red-tape bureaucracy made mistakes in names and figures. Thus, people whose allotted span of life had not yet run out might be summoned too soon before the infernal tribunal owing to the error of a careless scribe, and were then sent back to the world of the living. Others might escape taking their place among the dead due to the exemplary filial piety they had shown during their life or to the merit acquired by reciting the sacred texts of Buddhism or to their knowledge of magic formulae. This was how cases of total lethargy or of temporary death were explained. People who had recovered from such events had sometimes had the opportunity of stealing a glance at the lists on which was noted everyone's fate. They had found out from it how many years of life were left to them and at what age their relations and friends would die. Sometimes one of the dead with whom they were unacquainted had entrusted them with messages for parents and the information given by the shades below was found to be correct.

These descents to the lower regions and the prophetic revelations which resulted from them had provided, since T'ang times, one of the favourite themes of the various collections of "strange and wondrous tales."

The ordinary person lived surrounded by mysteries and supernatural beings. Marvels were part of his daily life, and anything and everything, in this world, might be a source of disquiet to him. His words and actions were circumscribed—temporarily for some things and permanently for others—by a multitude of restrictions and prohibitions. However much he might spare himself some possible misfortunes by consultation of almanacks and horoscopes and the prescriptions of geomancers, others were sure to turn up unexpectedly.

BUDDHISM AND TAOISM

In the thirteenth century the fervour had long gone out of Buddhism, but everywhere traces remained of the religious fever that China had experienced under the dynasties of North and South and under the T'ang, from the fifth to the ninth century. Almost all the important works of art of that period had been Buddhist: sanctuaries carved out of the sides of mountains, temples and towers for sacred relics, paintings, manuscript scrolls, bronze statues (sometimes covered in gold), stone statues, steles. In one of the gorges of the river Min in Szechwan the traveller still sees soaring up in front of him, at a point where a strong current sweeps his boat along, a colossal image of the divine Maitreya, carved out of the rock at the beginning of the eighth century. It is 324 feet high, has a head 30 yards in circumference, each eye measures 18 feet across, and it is surrounded by a wooden construction with thirteen storeys.

In Hangchow itself traces of the great period of Buddhism were not lacking, and there were still 57 Buddhist monasteries, large and small, within the ramparts, and 31 convents for nuns outside the city. Most of the Buddhist foundations, which amounted to a total of 385 in the two sub-prefectures centred in the town, were either situated within the urban area or near it; there were only 185 of them in the seven other districts belonging to the prefecture of Hangchow. The big monasteries endowed with official status were obliged to carry out ceremonies on behalf of the court. All of them performed the rites demanded of them by the faithful—usually funeral rites. The liturgy consisted of intoned recitation of sacred texts, Indian chants, and offerings of fruits, flowers and incense made to the Buddhas. There were lighted lamps at the foot of the statues. On festive days, the finest paintings and manuscripts possessed by the monastery were exhibited for the admiration of visitors. Streamers were hung in the great hall where rose, sometimes to a height of 30 feet, the cross-legged statues of the Buddhas with their smile, at once enigmatic and peaceful, which is the very image of the most perfect ataraxy. The most important festivals were those of the bathing of the statues on the 8th of the 4th moon, of the monks' return to the monasteries, where they remained confined for the summer months, on the 15th of the 4th moon, and the festival of the dead on the 15th of the 7th moon.

The whole of China had become permeated by Buddhism, but it had gone so deep that many people, even among the upper classes, were no longer conscious of it. The philosophers borrowed some of their ideas from Buddhism. They were no longer exclusively preoccupied with ethics and politics as their forerunners had been before the beginning of the Christian era, but tried to produce a philosophical system which would be a match for the Buddhist one. This need for a specifically Chinese philosophy made itself felt all the more sharply owing to the fact that Buddhism had ceased to be the main stimulus to intellectual life. Of the many Buddhist sects which were later to be perpetuated in Japan, the only one left was the school of dhyana (*zen* in Japanese), "a resurgence of mystical Taoism, particularly esteemed by artists and by the scholars."

In all classes, the Confucian ethic and Buddhist morality mingled indistinguishably. There were works that enjoyed an astonishing popularity in Sung times which provided each and every person with a means of calculating his merits and demerits according to a scale which gave positive or negative values for every single action, good or bad. One of these manuals, which in principle were of Buddhist inspiration, was so popular that, according to a calculation made at the beginning of the twentieth century, its distribution surpassed that of the Bible.

Let us briefly recall the essential principles of Buddhist doctrine, since it still provided numerous families among all sections of society with their articles of faith. The world is an illusion, a phantasmagoria. Life, resulting from our attachment to this unreal world, cannot be anything but a series of painful disappointments. Birth, illness, old age and death are all nothing but suffering. Only abstention from evil and the carrying out of pious acts will enable individuals, in the course of successive rebirths, to raise themselves in the hierarchy of beings and thus prepare the way for final deliverance.

To escape finally from the painful cycle of re-births a mystical revelation of the inner emptiness of this world was necessary. Religious practices (reading of sacred texts, abstinence from meat, worship of the Buddhas . . .) and pious works (gifts to monks and to Buddhist communities, contributions to festivals, construction of sanctuaries . . .) diminished one's stock of sins and increased one's stock of merits. A pious lay person would be re-born a human being in his or her next life, a sinner would be a dog, a pig, a demon, a shade. Intense faith or perhaps the recitation of a magic formula might save the believer at a moment of great peril. Finally, it was possible to intercede on behalf of the dead, and this was why Buddhist monks played such an important rôle in funeral ceremonies and in the cult of the dead: even people who were not practising Buddhists were moved by filial piety to have Buddhist religious services performed for their dead.

Like Buddhism, Taoism also had its monasteries, its communal organization, its sacred texts, its gods and saints, its liturgy. In all this, it had patterned itself upon its rival. But its communities were less rich, less numerous and less powerful than the Buddhist ones. Having a more definite slant towards magic, Taoism sought to prolong earthly life by means of a complex ascetic discipline as much physical as mental, and to transform the body into a more rarified and durable entity. The Taoist monks knew the secret of drugs for attaining Long Life, and being exorcists and makers of charms and amulets, they knew how to chase away demons and pestilences. But two contradictory tendencies can be distinguished among the Taoists of the twelfth and thirteenth centuries. One put the accent on the occult sciences, the other on ascetic disciplines. One of the most celebrated Taoists of the twelfth century, who was hostile to everything that smacked of magic in his religion, attempted a synthesis of the three "doctrines" (Buddhism, Taoism and Confucianism). According to him,

> man must realize in himself the natural wholeness which he has from Heaven by controlling his desires, particularly his sexual desires, which attach him to Earth and pollute his celestial nature; if his celestial nature is kept whole he can be sure of attaining Long Life and will ascend to Heaven among the Immortals.

Apart from Buddhism, which, in the course of centuries, had become completely integrated into the moral and religious thought of the Chinese, there was quite a large number of other foreign religions in thirteenth-century China. Nestorianism, a Christian heresy according to which the Virgin was not the mother of God but of a man, was introduced into China from Iran in the seventh century. It had practically disappeared by the tenth century, and it was only because of the Mongol conquest that it was reintroduced. But Marco Polo was to lament the fact that Christianity was so poorly represented in Hangchow. "There is," he said, "in so great a number of people no more than one church of Nestorian Christians only." This church was founded in 1279 or 1280, just after the Mongols had established themselves in South China. Manicheism, which also came from Iran, seems to have had a greater and more lasting success, although its influence was limited geographically—we have seen how, under the Sung, it inspired revolutionary sects in Fukien and Chekiang. On the other hand, Islam and Judaism, which for long were not distinguished from each other by the Chinese, never seem to have had any real influence in south-east China. They did not spread beyond the small foreign communities of Jews and, predominantly, Muslims, which existed in the big trading ports of China.

ASIAN CIVILIZATION

The Emergence of Modern Southeast Asia, edited by John Bastin
Modern China, edited by Albert Feuerwerker
Traditional China, edited by James T. C. Liu and Wei-ming Tu
Traditional India, edited by O. L. Chavarria-Aguilar
The Traditional Near East, edited by J. Stewart Robinson